400

DIETRICH BONHOEFFER
Selected Writings

D1502829

ALSO AVAILABLE FROM
HarperCollins*Publishers*

Love Letters from Cell 92
Dietrich Bonhoeffer and Maria von Wedemeyer

Dietrich Bonhoeffer: An Illustrated Biography
Eberhard Bethge

· FOUNT CLASSICS ·

DIETRICH BONHOEFFER

Selected Writings

Edited by Edwin Robertson

Fount
An Imprint of HarperCollins*Publishers*

Fount Paperbacks is an Imprint of
HarperCollins*Religious*
Part of HarperCollins*Publishers*
77–85 Fulham Palace Road, London W6 8JB

First published in Great Britain
in 1995 by Fount Paperbacks

1   3   5   7   9   10   8   6   4   2

Copyright © 1995 Edwin Robertson

Edwin Robertson asserts the moral right to be
identified as the compiler of this work

A catalogue record for this book is
available from the British Library

ISBN 0 00 627930-9

Printed and bound in Great Britain by
HarperCollinsManufacturing Glasgow

CONDITIONS OF SALE

This book is sold subject to the condition that it
shall not, by way of trade or otherwise, be lent, re-sold,
hired out or otherwise circulated without the publisher's
prior consent in any form of binding or cover other
than that in which it is published and without a
similar condition including this condition being
imposed on the subsequent purchaser.

All rights reserved. No part of this publication may be
reproduced, stored in a retrieval system, or transmitted,
in any form or by any means, electronic, mechanical,
photocopying, recording or otherwise, without the prior
permission of the publishers.

Contents

ACKNOWLEDGEMENTS

The author and publisher acknowledge the use of material from the publications mentioned in the Notes (pp.168ff).

Dietrich Bonhoeffer – A biography, Eberhard Bethge (1970, HarperCollins, London and San Francisco)

Love Letters from Cell 92, Dietrich Bonhoeffer and Maria von Wedemeyer (1994, HarperCollins, London and Abingdon Press, Nashville)

Extracts from the Collected Works of Dietrich Bonhoeffer (*Gesammelte Schriften*):

1. No Rusty Swords (1928–36)
2. The Way to Freedom (1935–39)
3. True Patriotism (1935–45)

(1965, 1966 and 1966 respectively, HarperCollins, London and San Francisco)

The Cost of Discipleship, (1959, SCM Press, London and Macmillan, New York)

Letters and Papers from Prison, (1971, enlarged edition, SCM Press, London and Macmillan, New York)

Introduction

Dietrich Bonhoeffer was born on 4 February 1906 in Breslau (then a German town, now Polish) a twin, born ten minutes before his sister, Sabine. They were a large family – eight children eventually, of whom the twins were sixth and seventh. In 1912 the family moved to Berlin on the appointment of Karl Bonhoeffer to the chair of psychiatry and neurology, the leading position in its field in Germany. A comfortable, academic family in Berlin they lived among academic neighbours on the edge of the Grünewald. Apart from his professorship, Karl Bonhoeffer was director of a psychiatric clinic called the *Charité*.

To the disappointment of the family, Dietrich chose to study theology and he had some of the finest teachers in the world: Adolf von Harnack in Berlin, neighbour and later teacher; the cream of Tübingen; and by reading only, Karl Barth. He was to remain a Barthian, although later he felt Karl Barth was not radical enough. He passed his examinations in Berlin and qualified as a lecturer; he did his initial pastoral work, first with a confirmation class in a poor suburb of Berlin and then as assistant minister to a German-speaking congregation in Barcelona.

After all that Germany could give him, Bonhoeffer studied in Union Theological Seminary in New York. There he learnt to admire the zeal of the black churches, and taught in the Abyssinian Church in Harlem.

He returned to Berlin, met Barth for the first time, and realized the growth of Nazism as a threat. Two days after Hitler came to power in 1933, Bonhoeffer broadcast an attack on the development of the Führer Prinzip (the idolizing of the leader) in youth work.

1

The broadcast was cut but he circulated the script. In the same year he attacked the Nazi treatment of the Jews in a powerful article, 'The Church and the Jewish Question'. He was from the start a marked man, but in the early days the high connections of his family protected him.

After joining the protests against the perversion of the Church's teaching by the Nazis, Bonhoeffer attempted to rouse the 'Confessing Church' (an organization of Protestant churches who defended the purity of doctrine against the perversion of the German Christians) to condemn the treatment of the Jews. When he failed to do this, he accepted an invitation to minister to the German-speaking congregations in London, where he served for two years, continuing his battle against Nazism and its influence in the churches. He persuaded almost every German-speaking congregation in Britain to support the Confessing Church against the German Christians. He was soon involved with the Ecumenical Movement and made the acquaintance of George Bell, the Bishop of Chichester. That relationship was the most important of his life – it was a father/son relationship and held unto death.

In 1935 Bonhoeffer returned to Germany to lead a theological seminary of the Confessing Church. With the Nazi State controlling universities, publishers, schools, etc., there was a need to train young men for the Church without Nazi contamination. The seminary was originally on the Baltic and eventually at Finkenwalde. From that base he repeatedly countered Nazi teaching and opposed any concession to it in the Church. The seminary was closed in 1937, and for a while Bonhoeffer remained in contact with his students, scattered throughout Pomerania. Then, when he saw the prospect of being called up for military service and knowing that he could not take the required oath to the Führer, he was persuaded to accept an invitation to America to lecture until the problem went away. That was in August 1939 and he knew almost immediately that he had made a mistake. His friends sought to rescue him, but he was convinced that, if war came, he must face it in Germany.

Bonhoeffer returned to find his family involved in a conspiracy to overthrow the Nazi government, which he was persuaded to join and thus avoid military service. The conspiracy was based in the centre of military intelligence (the *Abwehr*) which the Gestapo could not investigate. At first, he waited in the Benedictine Monastery at Ettal and felt useless and protected, but he was soon used to develop his contacts with the churches in neutral countries and to rescue Jews. The most daring action he had to take was a visit to Sweden to offer peace terms to the British, through the Bishop of Chichester. He was thus a double agent. It was not long before the cover of the *Abwehr* was blown and he was arrested among many others, some of his own family. He spent two years in prison. A few weeks before his arrest he had become engaged to Maria von Wedemayer, whose visits and letters were a great comfort to him. The conspiracy of which he was a part planned the assassination of Hitler and many attempts were made, though without success. When the last attempt was made, on 20 July 1944, he was in prison, though he awaited the result with anticipation. It failed, and like all the others Bonhoeffer was later executed.

While in prison, he read widely and thought through the problems of his Church. He fashioned a new and living theology, expressed largely through letters to his friend and close colleague, Eberhard Bethge. He wrote poems, drafted a play and started a novel. He looked forward to the time when he could write his new theology systematically in a book. He sent to Bethge a full outline of that book, but like his longed for marriage, it was never accomplished. He was put to death in Flossenbürg on 9 April 1945.

Bonhoeffer's letters have been studied together with his poems and prose writings in prison. Theologians have gone back to his earlier writings – two academic theses of great importance, *Sanctorum Communio* and *Act and Being*; a book containing the essence of his teaching at Finkenwalde, *The Cost of Discipleship*; an unfinished book on *Ethics*. In addition, smaller works have been published since, particularly *Life Together* and *Confession*. All these have helped to put the *Letters and Papers from Prison* in the context of a developing theology.

Dietrich Bonhoeffer was a biblical and systematic theologian. At thirty-nine, he cannot be said to have completed his work when it was interrupted by his cruel death. Throughout, he showed a sensitivity to events and tested his theological insights against the issues of his day. He saw evil as growing into a larger issue than traditional theology could handle. He was disappointed in his Church, whose theology had failed it in its time of trial. He found religious language inadequate and sought a new language, perhaps non-religious, 'but liberating and redeeming – as was Jesus' language; it will shock people and yet overcome them by its power; it will be the language of a new righteousness and truth, proclaiming God's peace with men and the coming of his kingdom'.

Edwin Robertson
December 1994

1

CHILDHOOD AND YOUTH

DEATH AND THE CHILD

Bonhoeffer liked thinking about death. Even in his boyhood he had liked imagining himself on his deathbed, surrounded by all who loved him, speaking his last words to them. Secretly he had often thought about what he would say at that moment. To him death was neither grievous nor alien. He would have liked to die young, to die a fine, devout death. He would have liked them all to see and understand that to a believer in God dying was not hard, but was a glorious thing. In the evening when he went to bed over-tired, he sometimes thought that it was going to happen. A slight sense of dizziness often alarmed him so much that he furiously bit his tongue, to make sure that he was alive and felt pain. Then, in his innocence, he cried out to God, asking to be granted a deferment. These experiences dismayed him to some extent. For obviously he did not want to die, he was a coward, his theatrical ideas disgusted him. And yet in moments of strength he often prayed that God might after all release him, for he was ready to die, and it was only his animal nature, which again and again made him contemptible in his own eyes, that led him astray from himself.

Then one day he had a grotesque idea. He believed himself to be suffering from the only incurable illness that existed, namely a crazy and irremediable fear of death. The thought that he would really have to die one day had such a grip on him that he faced the unalterable prospect with speechless fear. And there was no one who could free him from this illness because in reality it was no illness, but the most natural and obvious thing in the world, because it was the most

5

inevitable. He saw himself going from one person to another pleading and appealing for help. Doctors shook their heads and could do nothing for him. His illness was that he saw reality for what it was, it was incurable. He could tolerate the thought for only a few moments. From that day on he buried inside himself something about which for a long time he did not speak or think again. His favourite subject for discussion and for his imagination to dwell on had suddenly acquired a bitter taste. He spoke no more about a fine, devout death, and forgot about it.

(Bonhoeffer's memories of childhood trauma written down about 1932)[1]

THE AWFUL MOMENT OF DECISION

One day in the first form, when the master asked him what he wanted to study, he quietly answered 'theology', and flushed. The word slipped out so quickly that he did not even stand up. Having the teacher's gaze and that of the whole class directed at him personally, and not at his work, and being suddenly called upon to speak out like this, gave Bonhoeffer such conflicting feelings of vanity and humility that the shock led to an infringement of ordinary classroom behaviour, an appropriate expression of the consternation caused by the question and the answer. The master obviously thought so too for he rested his gaze on him for only a moment longer than usual, and then quickly and amiably released him, being nearly as disconcerted as his pupil. 'In that case you have more surprises to come', he said, speaking just as quietly. Actually the question 'For how long have you felt this?' had been on the teacher's lips, but as that would have touched on the secret of his own early, passionately begun but then quickly dropped study of theology – and also because he felt displeased with himself at having nothing better to say to a boy whom he had known and liked for a long time – he grew embarrassed, cleared his throat, and went back to the Greek text which was the subject of the lesson.

The boy absorbed that brief moment deep into himself. Something extraordinary had happened which he enjoyed yet at the same time felt ashamed of. Now they all knew, he had told them.

Now he was faced with the riddle of his own life. Solemnly he stood there in the presence of his God, in the presence of his class, the centre of attention. Did he look as he had wanted to look, serious and determined? He was filled with an unusual sense of well-being at the thought, though he immediately drove it away, realizing the grandeur of his confession and his task. Nor did it escape him that he had caused the master a certain embarrassment, though at the same time he had looked at Bonhoeffer with pleasure and approval. The moment swelled into pleasure, the classroom expanded into the infinite. There he stood in the midst of the world as the herald and teacher of his knowledge and ideals, they all had now to listen to him in silence, and the blessing of the Eternal rested upon his words and on his head! And again he felt ashamed. For he knew about his pitiful vanity. How often he had tried to master it; but it always crept back again, and it spoilt the pleasure of this moment. Oh, how well he knew himself at the age of seventeen, knowing all about himself and his weaknesses. And he realized that he knew himself well. Through the corner of that piece of self-knowledge his deep vanity again forced an entry into the house of his soul and made him afraid . . .

Why are you all looking at me like that? Why are you embarrassed, sir? Look away from me, for heaven's sake, denounce me as a mendacious, conceited person, who does not believe what he says. Don't keep so considerably silent, as if you understood me . . . A leaden silence lies over the throng, a dreadful silent mockery. No, it cannot be. He really is in earnest. They have no right to scorn him, they are doing him wrong, all of them. He prays: 'God, say yourself whether I am in earnest about you. Destroy me now if I am lying . . . They do not believe me. I know myself I am not good. But I know it myself and you, God, know it too. I do not need the others . . . I am with you. I am strong God, I am with you. Do you hear me? Or do you not? To whom am I speaking? To myself? To you? Do these others care? Who is it that is speaking, My faith or my vanity?'
(Bonhoeffer recalls his adolescent struggles in that same fragment of 1932) [2]

THE FASCINATION OF CATHOLIC ROME

I spent a lot of time with our priest from Bologna and let him explain a great deal to me. On Palm Sunday attended first mass in St Peter's, surrounded by a throng of seminarists, monks and priests of every conceivable shade of skin – the universality of the Church. In the evening, Vespers at Trinità del Monte. It had been a magnificent day; the first on which I gained some real understanding of Catholicism; no romanticism or anything of the sort, but I believe I am beginning to understand the concept of the Church . . .

Santa Maria Maggiore, all the confessionals occupied, with worshippers crowding around them. It is gratifying here to see so many anxious faces, to which all the things that are said against Catholicism do not apply. Children as well as adults confess with a real ardour which it is very moving to see. To many of these people confession is not an externally imposed 'must', but it has become an inner need. Confession does not necessarily lead to scrupulous living: often, however, that may occur and always will with the most serious people. Also it is not mere pedagogy, but to primitive people it is the only way of talking to God, while to the religiously more far-seeing it is the realization of the idea of the Church fulfilling itself in confession and absolution.

GOOD FRIDAY, FOUR OF FIVE HOURS
IN THE THRONG IN ST PETER'S

I had always hoped to have one more splendid experience in St Peter's . . . I had yet another last sight of what Catholicism is. In the afternoon I walked through the whole city, then I went by way of the Pantheon to throw my coin into the Trevi fountain . . . I must say that actual leaving was easier than the thought of it. I parted from most of it without sentimentality. When I looked at St Peter's for the last time there was a feeling of sadness in my heart and I quickly got into the tram and went away. Looking back, the papal audience had been a disappointment. The Pope made an indifferent impression. He was lacking in everything papal, in all *grandezza* . . .

After church with P. (the priest from Bologna), a long discussion, conducted vigorously on both sides. He tried to refute Kant, but involuntarily involved himself in the usual Catholic vicious circle. He accepts the validity of deducing the existence of God from the purposefulness of the universe, and, of course, in the process continually confuses logical knowledge with knowledge gained by faith, hence the vicious circle. He would very much have liked to convert me, and in his way is very genuinely convinced. But the method he used was the least likely to achieve his purpose – dialectical tricks that he does not use as such. The result of the discussion was a big withdrawal of sympathy on my part. Catholic dogma makes everything ideal depend upon Catholicism, without realizing it. There is a great difference between confession and the dogma of confession, also, unfortunately between 'church' and 'church dogmatics'.

Unification with Protestantism, however well it might become both sides, is, as I see it, out of the question. Catholicism will be able to do without Protestantism for a long time yet. The people are still very attached to it, and, in comparison with the ceremonial here on its tremendous scale, the Protestant Church looks like a small sect . . . Perhaps Protestantism should never have aimed at becoming an established church, but should have remained a big sect, for which things are always easier – and in that event it would perhaps not be in its present calamitous condition. An established Church believes it possesses an expansive capacity that enables it to give something to all. That it was able to do so at the time of its origin was eventually due to the political turn taken by questions which are no longer at issue today; and thus the more political circumstances have changed, the more it has lost its hold over the many; until finally the term Protestantism has come to conceal a great deal that frankly and honestly can be called nothing but materialism, with the result that the only thing about it that is valued and respected is the possibility of freedom of thought, to which the Reformers attached an entirely different meaning. Now, when the official tie between Church and State has been dropped (as it was under the Weimar Republic), the

Church is confronted with the truth; it has for too long been a home for homeless spirits, a place of refuge for uninformed edification. Had it never become an established Church, the state of affairs would be very different; it would still have no small number of enthusiastic supporters, in view of its size it would hardly be described as a sect, and it would present an unusual spectacle of religious life and piety; thus it would be the ideal form of religion for which there is so much search today . . . Perhaps a way of remedying the terrible plight of the Church presents itself here; it must begin to limit itself and make selections in every respect, particularly in the quality of its spiritual educators and what they teach; and in any event it must completely dissociate itself from the State as soon as possible . . . Is this a possible solution or is it not? Or is the whole game up? Will it shortly return to the bosom of the only saving Church, i.e. the Roman Church, under the semblance of fraternity? One would like to know.

[*From the diary kept in Rome, Holy Week, 1924*][3]

2

AMERICA: 1930–1931

SERMON TO AN AMERICAN CONGREGATION

Now I stand before you, not only as a Christian, but also as a German, who rejoices with his people and who suffers when he sees his people suffering, who confesses gratefully that he received from his people all that he has and is. So I bring you this morning a double message, the message of Germany and the message of Christianity in Germany. I hope you will hear the message with a Christian heart, with the readiness of a Christian soul to understand and to love, wherever and whenever it might be.

The 11th of November 1918 brought to Germany the end of a frightful and unparalleled time, a time which we pray, if God wills, will never return. For four years German men and lads stood for their home with an unheard of tenacity, and intrepidity, with the imperturbable consciousness of their duty, with an inexorable self-discipline and with a glowing love for their Fatherland, and with a belief in its future. For weeks and months these people suffered privations of every kind; they persevered in hunger and thirst, in pain and affliction, in craving after home, after mothers and wives and brothers and children. In the country the stream of tears of old and young people did not cease. Every day the message came to more than a thousand families that the husband, the father, the brother had died in a foreign country. Hardly any family was spared. (. . . I tell you from my personal experience, two brothers of mine stood at the front. The older one, 18 years old, was wounded, the younger one, 17 years old, killed. Three first cousins of mine were also killed, boys of 18 to 20 years old. Although I was then a small

11

boy I never can forget those most gloomy days of war.) Death stood at the door of almost every house and called for entrance. Once the message came about the death of many thousands of seventeen- and eighteen-year-old boys killed in a few hours. Germany was made a house of mourning. The breakdown could not be delayed much longer. Famine and enervation were too powerful and destructive.

I think you will release me from talking about our feelings in Germany in those days. The recollection of this time is gloomy and sad. Very seldom will you hear today in Germany anybody talking about those days. We will not reopen an old and painful wound. But however we felt, the war and its dreadful killing and dying was finished. Our minds were still too confused and bewildered; we could not yet conceive and quietly consider the meaning of all the events of the last years and months. But gradually we saw more and more clearly, and Christian people in Germany who took the course, and the end, of the war seriously, could not help seeing here a judgement of God upon this fallen world and especially upon our people.

Before the war we lived too far from God; we believed too much in our own power, in our almightiness and righteousness. We attempted to be a strong and good people, but we were too proud of our endeavour, we felt too much satisfaction with out scientific, economic and social progress, and we identified this progress with the coming of the kingdom of God. We felt too happy and complacent in this world; our souls were too much at home in this world. Then the great disillusionment came. We saw the impotence and weakness of humanity, we were suddenly awakened from our dream, we recognized our guiltiness before God and we humbled ourselves under the mighty hand of God. When I was speaking of 'guiltiness' I added on purpose, 'guiltiness *before God*'. Let me tell you frankly that no German and no stranger who knows well the history of the origin of the war believed that Germany bears the sole guilt of the war — a sentence which we were compelled to sign in the Treaty of Versailles. (The Allied and Associated Governments affirm and Germany accepts the responsibility of Germany and her allies for causing all the loss and damage to which the Allied and Associated

Governments and their nations have been subjected as a consequence of the war imposed upon them by the aggression of
Germany and her allies.) I personally do not believe, on the other
hand, that Germany was the only guiltless country. But as a
Christian I see the main guilt of Germany in quite a different light. I
see it in Germany's complacency, in her belief in her almightiness, in
the lack of humility and faith in God and fear of God. It seems to me
that this is the meaning of the war for Germany; we had to recognize
the limits of man and by that means we discovered anew God in his
glory and mightiness, in his wrath and his grace.

The same 11th of November 1918 which brought to us the end of
the war, was the beginning of a new epoch of suffering and grief. The
first years after the war showed to us the corruption of our public life.
The general poverty caused by the hunger blockade had dreadful
consequences. Germany was starved out. (...The consequences of
the blockade were frightful. I myself in those years was a schoolboy
and I can assure you that not only I had in those days to learn what
hunger means. I should wish that you would have to eat this food for
only one day that we had for three or four years, and I think you
would get a glimpse of the privation which Germany had to endure.
Put yourself in the situation of the German mothers whose husbands
were disabled or were killed in the war, and who had to provide for
growing hungry children. Countless tears were shed in these last
years of the war and the first years of peace by the desperate mothers
and hungry children. As a matter of fact, instead of a good meal there
was largely sawdust in our bread, and the fixed portion for every day
was five or six slices of that kind of bread. You could not get any butter
at all. Instead of sugar we had saccharin tablets. The substitute for
meat, fish, vegetables, even for coffee, jam and toast — were turnips
for breakfast, lunch and supper. Germany really was starved out.
Thousands and thousands of old and young people, of little children,
died simply because there was not enough to eat. Fatal epidemics ran
through the country. The *grippe* of 1919 demanded more than a
hundred victims. People were too enervated and could not resist.
When the wintertime came we had not enough coal for heating our

rooms. We had no cloth for our clothes; it is no exaggeration to say that many people had to buy suits made more of paper than of real cloth. In the street you could see the undernourished and poorly dressed people, the pale and sick children. The number of suicides increased in a terrifying way. I remember very well that on the walk to my school I had to pass by a bridge, and in the winters from 1917 to 1919 almost every morning when I came to this bridge I saw a group of people standing by the river, and everybody who passed by knew what had happened. These impressions were hard for young boys.)

I will stop picturing these frightful months and years. But before I go on, I will not forget to tell you that the Quaker congregations of the States were the first who after the war in an admirable work supported the German children. Many thousand children were saved from starvation. Germany remembers in deep thankfulness this work of love of the Quaker society. . . .

(. . . there was one wound which was much more painful than all these privations and needs, that was Article 231 of the Treaty of Versailles. I will tell you frankly, that this is the wound which still is open and bleeds in Germany. I will try to explain to you briefly what our attitude towards this question was and is. When the war broke out the German people did not consider very much the question of guilt. We thought it to be our duty to stand for our country and we believed of course in our essential guiltlessness. You cannot expect in such a moment of excitement an objective and detached evaluation of the present conditions. The war has its own psychology. The German soldiers stood in the war in the confident faith in the right-eousness of their country. But already during the war you could hear in Germany some sceptical voices; who can tell who is wrong and who is right? We all fight for our country and believe in it, Germans no less than French. Now, twelve years after the war the whole question has been thoroughly searched historically. I personally see many faults in our policy before the war. I am not going to defend my country in every point. But a study of the diplomatic documents of Belgium of the years before the war, for instance, shows irrefutably that other countries had committed the same or greater faults than

Germany. It can be proved historically that Article 231 of the Treaty of Versailles is an injustice against our country and we have a right to protest. That fact is recognized by the largest parts of educated people in Europe and in America.)

Everyone who is familiar with the conditions in Germany today, twelve years after the war, knows that in spite of some changes in their external aspect, social conditions are almost as unhappy as ten or twelve years ago. The debts of the war press upon us, not only with regard to our financial standard, but likewise in regard to our whole behaviour; we see the hopelessness of our work. It is impossible for us to provide social and economic conditions for our children of the future in which we can trust for security. The Germans are a suffering people today, but they will not despair. They will work for building up a new and better home, they will work for peace in their country, they will work for peace in the world. When I came over here, I was astonished on being asked again and again, what German people think about a future war. I tell you the truth: German people do not speak at all about that; they don't even think of it. You almost never hear in Germany talk about war and much less about a future war. We know what a war means for a people.

I have been accustomed once in every year since my boyhood to wander on foot through our country, and so I happen to know many classes of German people very well. Many evenings I have spent with the families of peasants around the big stove, talking about the past and future, about the next generation and their chances. But always when the talk happened to touch war, I observed how deep the wound was which the past war had caused to everyone. The German people need and want above all peace. (...They want to work peacefully in their fields, they fear any disturbance. But it is no different among other classes in Germany. In the working class, for instance, started the German peace movement, and the interest for international trade makes these people naturally pacifistic. It was in Germany that the thought arose that the workers in France and in Germany are closer to one another than the various classes within each country. You will find large worker organizations with a partic-

ularly pacifistic programme, especially also the Christian organizations of workers. The bourgeois in Germany had to bear the hardest
burden after the war, but nevertheless I can assure you that by far the
most of them would abominate a war more than anything else. You
might be interested in hearing something about the attitude of the
youth towards war and peace. The youth movement which started
immediately after the war was in its tendencies entirely pacifist. In a
deep religious feeling we recognized all people as brothers, as children of God. We wanted to forget all hard and bitter feelings after
the war. We had anew discovered a genuine and true love for our
home country, and that helped us to get a great and deep feeling for
other people, for all mankind. You see there are many various
motives working for peace, but whatever motive it might be there is
one great aim and one great work; the peace movement in Germany
is an enormous power.)

As a Christian minister I think that just here is one of the greatest
tasks for our church: to strengthen the work of peace in every
country and in the whole world. It must never more happen that a
Christian people fights against a Christian people, brother against
brother, since both have one Father. Our churches have already
begun this international work. But more important than that is, it
seems to me, that every Christian man and woman, boy and girl take
seriously the great idea of the unity of Christianity, above all
personal and national desires, of the one Christian people in the
whole world, of the brotherhood of mankind, of the charity about
which Paul says: 'Charity suffereth long and is kind; charity envieth
not; charity vaunteth not itself, is not puffed up, beareth all things,
believeth all things, hopeth all things. Charity never faileth.' Let us
consider that the judgement comes for every man and woman, boy
and girl in America and Germany, in Russia and in India, and God
will judge us according to our faith and love. How can the man who
hates his brother expect grace from God? That is my message as a
German and as a Christian to you: let us love one another, let us
build in faith and love one holy Christianity, one brotherhood with
God the Father, and Christ the Lord, and the Holy Spirit as the

sanctifying power. Nobody is too little or too poor for this work; we need every will and force. I address now especially you, boys and girls of the United States, future bearers and leaders of the culture of your country. You have brothers and sisters in our people and in every people; do no forget that. Come what may, let us never more forget that one Christian people is the people of God, that if we are in accord, no nationalism, no hate of race or classes can execute its designs, and then the world will have its peace for ever and ever. (. . . This is my message for you: hear the voice of your German brothers and sisters, take their stretched out hand. We know it is not enough only to talk and to feel the necessity of peace; we must work seriously. There is so much meanness, selfishness, slander, hatred, prejudice among the nations. But we must overcome it. Today, as never before, nations of Europe — except Germany — are preparing for war. This makes our work very urgent. We must no longer waste time. Let us work together for an everlasting peace.) Let us remember the prayer of Christ spoken shortly before his end: 'I pray for them which shall believe in me; that they all may be one; as thou, Father, art in me, and I in thee, that they also may be one in us.'

And the peace of God which passeth all understanding, shall keep your hearts and minds through Christ Jesus. Amen.

At this time there comes to my mind an evening, which I spent not a long time ago with a group of young people from our German youth movement. It was a glorious summer night. We were outdoors far away from the noise and bustle of the city on the top of a mountain, above us the sky with its millions of stars, the quietness of the evening, below us the lights of the villages, the misty fields and the black woods; not one of us spoke a word. We heard nothing but the peaceful rustling of the brooks and the trees. On that evening a great and deep love came anew into our hearts, a love for our home and for the starry sky. The boys had carried branches of trees and lit a big fire on the top of the mountain and while we were staring into the blazing fire in silence, a boy began to speak about his love for his country and for the starry sky, which at that very time was shining upon all mankind, and he said: 'How wonderful it would be if people of all nations lived in peace and quiet as the stars in the heaven above, if only all nations could live together like brothers as they do in their own country.' When he finished all the boys and girls raised their hands as a sign that they were willing to work for this peace for everyone in his place, for the peace in the country and the world. Then we sat down and while the fire was burning out we sang our most beautiful folk songs about the love of our country and the peace of all mankind. With the deep understanding of our great task before us we went home.

More than a year has passed since that time and I wish to bring this message from my German students to the students of this great country.

[*An English sermon preached several times in the U.S.A., 1931*][1]

RECALLING AN EARLY ROMANCE

'Listen Maria, I want to tell you something. I'm much older than you. I, too, have known that insensate, heady, uncertain desire in my time. It was never fulfilled. I was once in love with a girl; she became a theologian; and our paths ran parallel for many years. She was about my age. I was twenty-one when it began. We didn't realize we loved each other. More than eight years went by. Then we discovered the truth from a third person, who thought he was helping us. We then discussed the matter frankly, but it was too late. We had evaded and misunderstood each other for too long. We could never be entirely in sympathy again, and I told her so. Two years later she married, and the weight on my mind gradually lessened. We never saw or wrote to each other again. I sensed at that time that, if I ever got married, it could only be to a much younger girl, but I thought that impossible, both then and thereafter. Being totally committed to my work for the Church in the ensuing years, I thought it not only inevitable but right that I should forgo marriage altogether.'

[*Letter to Maria von Wedemayer, 19 May 1944*][2]

3

THE INFLUENCE OF
KARL BARTH

THE FIRST MEETING

Bonn, 15 July 1931: Here I am sitting in the park in front of the University. Barth lectures this morning at seven. I had a short talk with him. This evening there is a discussion evening in his home with people from Maria Laach (a Benedictine monastery, near to Bonn, where the biblical and liturgical renewal of the Catholic Church was evident as early as 1914). I am looking forward to it immensely. Despite your thorough preparation there was a great deal in the lecture that surprised me. Besides, he looked terrifying. Does he always?

Bonn, 24 July 1931: Hans Fischer has just gone. I have reread the last two pages of Barth's 'Ethics' II, from Barth's lecture notes . . . You will well be able to imagine that I have often wished that you were here, particularly so that you could have a good laugh at the pundits. I don't dare do that so much here (that sounds improbable doesn't it?), but with my bastard theological derivation I have less occasion, as I noticed again quite clearly. They have a sharp scent for thoroughbreds here. No negro passes for 'white'; they even examine his fingernails and the soles of his feet! Up till now they've been showing me hospitality as the unknown stranger. Now with Karl Barth himself, of course, everything is completely different. One breathes in an orderly way, one is no longer afraid of dying of suffocation in this thin air. I don't think that I have regretted anything that I have failed to do in my theological past as much as the fact that I did not come here earlier. Now there are only three weeks for me to be here – seminars, meetings, an open evening and yesterday a couple of hours lunch with Barth . . . it is important and surprising to see how Barth stands over and beyond his books. There is an openness with him, in readiness for any objection which should hit the mark, and along with this such concentration and impetuous insistence upon the point, whether it is made arrogantly or modestly, dogmatically or completely uncertainly, and not only when it serves his own theology. I am coming to understand more and more why Barth's writings are so difficult to understand. I have been impressed even more with discussions with him than by his writings and his lectures. For he is really all there. I have never seen anything like it before and wouldn't have believed it possible.

My visit to him yesterday, which I was really rather hesistant about, especially as I knew how busy he was, was just such an occasion as you have described to me.

We very soon came to the problem of ethics and had a long discussion. He would not make concessions to me where I expected he would have had to. Beside the one great light in the night, he said, there were also many little lamps, so-called 'relative ethical critieria'; he could not, however, make their significance and application and nature comprehensible to me – we didn't get beyond his reference to the Bible. Finally he thought that I was making grace into a principle and killing everything else with it. Of course I disputed his first point and wanted to know why everything else should not be killed. Had you been there we would have had a third front and perhaps a great deal might have become clearer. But I was glad to be able for once to hear Barth's position in detail. He then went on to speak of a great many other things, and he urged me to develop the small work on the delimitation of Catholicism in contemporary theology about which I have already spoken to you.

During our conversation there were many real *bons mots* but they would be too feeble to repeat. Eventually after a hard struggle I went home. Today I have been invited for the evening to a group of Barth's closest pupils, and after that there is a meeting. Then next Tuesday it's all over. I don't look forward to going home.

Berlin, 8 October 1931: Gogarten gave a lecture on ethics which had a couple of good formulations, but was received by the people here – they are pedants – with scorn and indignation; he spoke for three hours with a pause for ten minutes! I was again surprised to see how great the difference is between him and Barth. I would not feel particularly drawn to Breslau, but I would go to Bonn again any day. That was really an extraordinary time!
[*Extracted from the letters to his Swiss friend, Erwin Sutz, 1931*][1]

4

A PASTOR IN BERLIN

A HARVEST FESTIVAL SERMON

'For thy goodness is better than life' (Psalm 63:3)

Two and a half millenia have now passed since the ancient Jewish saint, far from Jerusalem and his homeland, devoured by misery in body and soul, surrounded by mockers and enemies of his God, pondered the strange and wonderful ways God had led him. It was no easy, peaceful meditation. It was a struggle for meaning in life, a struggle for faith in God. The pillars of life had crumbled away. Where he expected to find a firm foothold, he found nothing but emptiness. 'God, where art thou? God, who am I? My life falls crashing down into the bottomless abyss. God I am afraid, where is thy goodness? And yet thou art my God and thy goodness is better than life.' Here is one of those sayings which do not let a man go again once he has understood it. Its gentle gleam is deceptive; inwardly it is a hard saying, full of passion conceived in the conflict of two different worlds, the world of the Bible in conflict with our own.

'Thy goodness is better than life': it is the triumphant cry of the distressed and abandoned, of the weary and overburdened, the cry of longing uttered by the sick and the oppressed; the song of praise among the unemployed and the hungry in the great cities; the prayer of thanksgiving prayed by tax-gatherers and prostitutes, by sinners known and unknown. But is it really that? No, it is not, not in our world, not in our age. It is only true for the unreal world of the Bible, which frightens and scandalizes us with its strangeness. Or perhaps

22

the verse does not seem so particularly remarkable after all. Perhaps we think that it is perfectly self-evident. These things have become part of the life of a Christian. If that is how we think, we shall have to discover what the Psalmist is really saying here, and, whether it really is so obvious.

At some point in our Psalmist's life something quite decisive happened: God came into his life. From that moment his life was changed. I don't mean that suddenly he became good and pious — it may well be that he was that before God came. But now God had come and had drawn near to him, and that fact alone made his life remarkable. It completely tore him apart. We so often hear and say that religion makes men happy and harmonious and peaceful and content. Maybe that's true of religion but it is not true of God and his dealing with men. It is utterly wrong. This is what the Psalmist discovered. Something had burst open inside him, he was divided by the struggle burning within him, which every day became more and more heated and terrible. From hour to hour, he came to feel that his old beliefs were being torn from him. He struggled desperately to hold on to them; but God had taken them from him and would never give them back. As God conquers him, he resists the more firmly and desperately, holding on to what is left; but the more firmly he holds on to what he has, the harder must God strike to break it free, and the more it hurts when it is torn away. And so the breathless struggle goes on, with God the victor and man defeated; he no longer knows where it will all lead to and he sees that he is lost; he does not know whether he hates or loves the one who has forced his way so violently into his life and destroyed his peace. He struggles for every inch and in despair yields to the weapons of God. And his position would not be quite so hopeless were it not for the fact that God's weapons are so strange and wonderful, that they cast down and lift up, that they wound and yet heal, that they kill and yet bring life; God speaks: 'If you want my mercy, then let me have victory over you; if you want my life then let me hate and destroy that which is evil in you, if you want my goodness, then let me take your life.' And now it has come to the final struggle. Everything has been surrendered up and only one thing has been left to the man, which he is determined to hold on to: his life. Still God will not call a halt, but storms this last citadel of all. And so the battle rages on for the last thing which he has; the man defends himself like a madman. God cannot want this, God is not cruel. God is good and kind. And yet the answer comes back: 'If you want my goodness then give me the last thing you have, give me your life. Now choose!'

Such heights terrify us; it is as if someone led us to the limits of the world and as if we looked down into an abyss and he said: 'Now jump!' We feel as if we had been torn apart. How can we choose between God's goodness and our life? What is our life? Everything that we perceive, hear, taste, feel; everything which surrounds us, which we possess, which we are used to, which we love. What is God's goodness? In any case something which we cannot see, cannot perceive and grasp and indeed cannot believe; something which we do not possess, something quite improbable, something outside this world, standing over and above all events, and yet which speaks to us so directly. Who would dare to make a free choice here? God himself must win the victory, and it seems humanly impossible that we should now hear from the Psalmist's lips the words: 'God, thou art my God. Thy goodness is better than life.'

Some of you will now be indignant and you will begin to object. What sort of exaggerated and wild talk is this? You can't talk about the goodness of God in that way. That I'm in good health, that I've still got food and drink to share with my family, that I've got work and a house, that's what God's goodness means to me and that's what I should thank him for. But I neither know nor understand anything of this struggle with God's goodness.

My friends, today is harvest festival, and a very proper time for us to reflect seriously about what God's goodness means to us. Unmoved by the bitter worries and unrest of our time, nature goes about her work in the world. She produces food for the peoples of the earth. When she withholds her gifts, millions die; when she bestows them lavishly, mankind flourishes. No man has control over her and when he is confronted by her power, man grows silent and is reminded of him who has the power over nature. Today we celebrate the harvest festival in particular circumstances with specific thoughts in mind. The harvest has not brought us what we hoped for. Every hour of rain in August and September, meant hours of hunger and privation in the coming winter for hundreds of children and adults. This has already caused us great sorrow. But on top of this comes one of the worst plagues which can ever be afflicted on a people, and which now moves over the whole world: unemployment. We must be prepared for the fact that this winter seven million people in Germany will find no work, which means hunger for fifteen or twenty million people. Another twelve million or more in England, twenty or more in America, while at this very moment sixteen million are starving in China, and the position is not much better in India. These are the bold statistics behind which stands a terrible reality. Should we overlook these millions of people when we celebrate our harvest festival in church? We dare not. They challenge all we say.

When we sit down this evening to a full table and say grace, and thank God for his goodness, we shall not be able to avoid a strange feeling of uneasiness. It will seem incomprehensible to us that we should be the ones to receive such gifts, and we will be overwhelmed by such thoughts and will think that we have not in any way deserved these gifts more than our hungry brothers in our town. What if precisely at the moment when we are thanking God for his goodness towards us, there is a ring at the door, as so often happens these days, and we find someone standing there who also wants to thank God for some small gift, but to whom such a gift has been denied and who is starving with his children and who will go to bed in bitterness? What becomes of our grace in such moments? Will we really feel like saying that God is merciful to *us* and angry with *him*, or that the fact that we still have something to eat proves that we have won a special position of favour in God's sight, that God feeds his favourite children and lets the unworthy go hungry? May the merciful God protect us from the temptation of such an attitude. May he lead us to a true understanding of his goodness. Don't we see that the gifts of his goodness become a curse for us if we have such thoughts about them and act in such a way, if we look at ourselves, instead of growing humble in our richness as we consider the unexplained mystery of God and the need which surrounds us, and if we thank God only for his goodness to us instead of becoming conscious of the immeasureable responsibility which is laid upon us by his goodness? If we want to understand God's goodness in his gifts, then we must think of them as in trust for our brothers. Let no one say: 'God has blessed me with money and possessions' and then live as if he and his God were alone in the world. For the time will come when he realizes that he has been worshipping the idols of his good fortune and his selfishness. Possessions are not God's blessing and goodness, but the opportunities of service which he entrusts to us.

This has already brought us some distance along the way towards understanding what God's goodness is. Whoever has a task lain upon him by God sees himself set between two worlds, between the world of God and the world of his neighbour. From God we hear the words: 'If you want my goodness to stay with you then serve your neighbour, for in him God comes to you himself'; such a man sees in his neighbour the material and spiritual need he is called to meet. And now the struggle is played out of which the Psalmist speaks. 'If you want my mercy, then give your neighbour a share in your possessions. If you want my love then give your neighbour your soul. If you want my goodness then stake your life for your neighbour. And if you don't do all this then that which was God's goodness to you, the gifts which he showered on your body and soul, will turn into a curse on you.' Which of us would care to say that he had done all this, that in his thoughts and particularly in his actions he had really understood God's goodness? It is already a great deal if we have even understood that God's goodness leads us into a struggle, that it is not something which we receive and then simply possess, so that we live on, somewhat happier, somewhat richer, but essentially unaltered. But how miserably we enter on this struggle; with so little passion and with so much fear, weakness, trembling and sadness; and how little does it really take hold of the roots of our being. Yet we shall not understand this struggle at all until we understand how radical and basic it is. 'Thy goodness is better than life', does not just mean better than your house, than your food, than your work, than your reputation, than your humour, than your physical, artistic and spiritual pleasures, than your wife and children, but it means more than all that; it means that it is better than the one thing you still have when you have lost everything, better than your life. Which of us has really admitted that God's goodness leads us into a conflict, which involves the physical side of our life, and not only that also, our work, our honour and even our family? Who would allow himself to be drawn into such conflicts, and who would see God's goodness in such conflicts? And above all, who sees that we have not grasped the meaning of God's goodness until the conflict goes much deeper and seizes hold of our life and reaches out beyond even that?

Let us take an example. There are two people who love each other. One says to the other: 'Tell me how much you love me.' And the other replies: 'For your love I would leave all my friends, all my fortune.' 'Is that all?' 'For your love I would sacrifice my reputation and my honour.' 'Is that the limit of your love?' 'For your love I would leave brothers and friends. Oh, if only I can have you ... for your love I would give everything that I have.' 'Even the last thing that you have? Would you give it for my love?' 'You mean would I give my life for your love? What a contradiction, how can I enjoy your love without my life? — And yet your love is more, your love is better than my life!'

Who would hesitate to admire the strength of such words, who would not be proud that men are capable of such words? But will not every Christian be struck with terror in his heart when he makes the great comparison that we are thinking of now? How is it that human passion is capable of such uncanny efforts in its struggle for the person it loves, and that we, when it is a question of God's love, when in other words something quiet different is at stake, are helpless? See how joyfully the lover stakes his possessions, his happiness, his honour and his life for his loved one, how he is never short of ideas for something new to offer up to his love, just as no price seems to him too high to pay to possess the love of the other ... and see how miserable our deeds and thoughts for God's love are, when we think that we have done enough for God's love by dropping a few coppers into the collection, by putting on a slightly brighter face and by acting a little more peaceably. Why with us does the fire always go out right at the beginning while over there it burns so brightly? Is that Christian life? Is that how Jesus Christ's life has been painted to us? O God, it's because we no longer know you, because we no longer seek you, because we no longer know what madness it is to live and not to think of you, who stand at the beginning and end of our life and judge us in eternity! Because we no longer look at God's love in Jesus Christ and no longer allow him to stir us into new life. Because we cling to ourselves and want to stand alone, because we cannot believe that it is God alone who can bear us up and who can give an eternal purpose to our life, even if outwardly it is dashed to pieces. We have sinned against God's unique honour and mercy. We have become guilty in his eyes! God gives us a task to perform and we fail, because we cling more to ourselves than to God! God asks how much our love for him is worth and we answer: 'Less than our own.' And so we cast God's goodness out of our lives.

But now comes the greatest wonder that the world has ever known. In the very place where we have fallen away from God, where we have become dead and unreceptive to him, in our guilt, God's goodness searches us out, and he reveals himself to us once again as the eternal promise of God, in Jesus Christ, which far surpasses all guilt and all life. Only the man who in the darkness of guilt, of unfaithfulness, of enmity towards God, has felt himself touched by the love which never ceases, which forgives everything and which points beyond all misery to the world of God, only such a man really knows what God's goodness means.

But of course we are not lifted out of life. Our task still remains with us and we are continually asked by God: 'What is my love worth to you?' But the more deeply we recognize what God's goodness is, the more lively our answer will be, and again we shall be led by God's goodness to perform our task and will be brought to him again through our acknowledged guilt. When will the time come that, at least in the Christian community, the world of our Psalmist will break in and in happiness or in misery, in hunger or in sickness, in fear or trouble, in sadness or guilt, in good or bad harvest we can make a truly joyful thanksgiving:

> And though they take our life,
> Goods, honour, children, wife,
> Yet is their profit small;
> These things shall vanish all:
> The City of God remaineth!

O God, thy goodness is better than life — Amen.

[*Preached in Berlin, 4 October 1931*][1]

THE CONFIRMATION CLASS

Tomorrow there's the examination for the confirmation candidates. Confirmation in a fortnight. I have devoted almost all of the second half of the seminar to the candidates. Since New Year I've been living here in north Berlin so as to be able to have the young men up here every evening, in turns of course! We eat supper and then we play something — I've introduced them to chess, which they now play with great enthusiasm. In principle anyone can come, even unannounced. And they all love coming. So I don't have to go over-straining them. Then at the end of the evening I read them something from the Bible and after that we have a short spell of catechising, which often becomes very serious. The instruction went in such a way that I can hardly tear myself away from it. Of course the young men are often quite dim, but I've sometimes been delighted. It has really been possible to talk to them and they have listened, often with mouths wide open. It is something new to them to be given something other than learning the catechism. I have developed all my instructions on the idea of the community, and these young men, who are always listening to party political speeches, know quite well what I'm getting at. But they see unbeliev-ably clearly what the limitations are, so that again and again when we are talking about the Holy Spirit in the community, the objection comes, 'But surely it's not like that at all. In all these things the Church is far behind the political youth organization or sports club. We feel at home in the club, but in the church?' — And again and again we have found our way from faith in the communion of saints to the forgiveness of sins, and I believe that they have now grasped something of it. Nothing sudden has happened, except perhaps that they were paying full attention at this point and doing so of their own accord. But perhaps the foundation has been laid for something which will grow slowly. Perhaps!

I also had some very serious conversations with individual young people. I am reluctant to confess it, but it is true that I never made any detailed preparation for the classes. Of course I had the stuff there, but then I simply went on; first I chatted with the young people for a couple of minutes and then I began. I was not afraid of preaching to the children quite simply, and I believe that in the end anything else is pedagogic doctrinairism. They have only to be taught enough for them to understand the sermon. Then one must begin to talk oneself, quite regardless, and then I found in my own case — I don't know why I did — that here the straight biblical material and references to the great hope which we have, appeared time and time again in sermons like this. And it was just at these points that the young people paid most attention, even if such a sermon lasted more than half an hour. As a contrast to this there are my worst experiences in visiting their homes. I sometimes, indeed often, stand there and think that I would have been well equipped to do such visits if I had studied chemistry. It sometimes seems to me that all our work comes to grief on the care of souls. To think of those excruciating hours or minutes when I or the other person try to begin a pastoral conversation, and how haltingly and lamely it goes on! And in the background there are always the ghastly home condi-tions, about which one really cannot say anything. Some people tell one about their most dubious way of life without any misgivings and in a free and easy way, and one feels that if one were to say something then they simply wouldn't understand. In short, it is a very troubled chapter, and I sometimes try to console myself by thinking that this sort of pastoral care is something which just wasn't there before. But perhaps it is really the end of our Christianity that we fail here. We have learnt to preach again, at least a little bit, but the care of souls?

[*An account of the Confirmation classes in Wedding, Berlin, in a letter to Erwin Sutz, 26 February 1932*][2]

5

THEOLOGICAL THOUGHTS
ON THE WORLD ALLIANCE

THEOLOGY OF THE ECUMENICAL MOVEMENT

There is still no theology of the ecumenical movement. As often in history as the Church of Christ has reached a new understanding of its nature, it has produced a new theology appropriate to this self-understanding. A change in the Church's understanding of itself is proved authentic by the production of a theology. For theology is the Church's self-understanding of its own nature on the basis of its understanding of the revelation of God in Christ, and this self-understanding of necessity always begins where there is a new trend in the Church's understanding of itself. If the ecumenical movement stems from a new self-understanding of the Church of Christ, it must and will produce a theology. If it does not succeed in this, that will be evidence that it is nothing but a new and up-to-date improvement in church organization. No one requires a theology of such an organization, but simply quite definite concrete action in a concrete task. There is no theology of the 'Midnight Mission' (social work amongst tramps and prostitutes). But it is very important to us that in comparison the ecumenical movement is something completely different. It would be wrong to say that it was the work of the Faith and Order conference at Lausanne (World Conference on Faith and Order, Lausanne, 1927) to produce a theology of the ecumenical movement. We must rather ask on what basis did the conference at Lausanne do its theological work together? Was this in itself an expression of the Church's new self-understanding or was it in the last resort a work of expediency aimed at the better understanding of different theological terminologies? Depending on the answer, we will know what we may and what we may not expect of Lausanne. Without doubt ecumenical work is here most closely bound up with practical work. As a result, until now, a large group of men experienced in practical work have looked with some disregard on the work of theology. 'Thank God we don't have to bother about theology here. We are at last free from those problems which so hamper Christian action.' That is what they have been saying. But just this attitude has become dangerous and demands our fullest protest; for it has had as its most perceptible consequence the exposing of ecumenical work to politically determined trends. Because there is no theology of the ecumenical movement, ecumenical thought has become powerless and meaningless among German youth at present, because of the political surge of nationalism. And the situation is scarcely different in other countries. There is no theological anchorage which holds while the waves dash in vain from right and left. Now there is great helplessness and the confusion of concepts is boundless. Any one engaged in ecumenical work must suffer the charges of being unconcerned with the Fatherland. And why is all this? Only because we have neglected to work out clear theological lines at the right time, lines along which ecumenical work should progress. I have nothing against the practical contribution of the Church in ecumenical work! Here we have every occasion for thankfulness and respect. But what is it that has emerged time and time again with rudimentary force at the international youth conferences of recent times? What gave these conferences so little 'practical' character, what put them against the traditional form of resolutions? It is the recognition of the deep helplessness that there is precisely in those questions which should be the basis of our being together. What is this Christianity which we always hear mentioned? Is it essentially the content of the Sermon on the Mount, or is it the message of the reconciliation in the cross and the resurrection of our Lord? What significance does the Sermon on the Mount have for our actions? And what is the significance of the message of the cross? What is the relationship between the forms of our modern life and the Christian proclamation? What has the state, business, our social life to do with Christianity? It is undeniable that here we must all still confess our ignorance, and it is equally undeniable that we should recognize this our ignorance as our fault. We really *should* know more here. We have neglected to think clearly and decisively and to take up a firm attitude. And only now, when we are in the middle of the lake, do we notice that the ice on which we are standing is breaking up. For us, this clearly means that the position that has been recognized here must not be concealed again. No good at all can come from acting before the world and oneself as though we knew the truth, when in reality we do not. This truth is too important for that, and it would be a betrayal of the truth if the Church were to hide itself behind resolutions and pious so-called Christian principles, when it is called to look the truth in the face and once and for all confess its guilt and its ignorance. Indeed, some resolutions can have nothing complete, nothing clear about them unless the whole seriousness of the whole Christian truth, as the Church knows it or confesses that it does not know it, stands behind them. Qualified silence might perhaps be more appropriate for the Church today than talk which is possibly very unqualified. That means protest against any form of the Church which does not honour the question of truth above all things.

The concern of youth deeply involved in ecumenical work is this: How does our ecumenical work, or the work of the World Alliance, look in the mirror of the truth of the Gospel? And we cannot approach such questions in any other way than by new, strict theological work on the biblical and Reformation basis of our ecumenical understanding of the Church, in complete seriousness and without regard for its consequences or its success. We ask for a responsible theology of the ecumenical movement for the sake of the truth and the certainty of our cause.

Our work in the World Alliance is based – consciously or unconsciously – on a quite definite view of the Church. The Church as the one community of the Lord Jesus Christ, who is Lord of the world, has the commission to say his Word to the whole world. The territory of the one Church of Christ is the whole world. Each individual church has geographical limits drawn to its own preaching, but the *one* church has no limits. And the churches of the World Alliance have associated themselves together the better to be able to express this their claim to the whole world, or rather this claim of their Lord's to the whole world. They understand it as the task of the Church to make the claim of Jesus Christ clear to the whole world. And this includes the repudiation of the idea that there are divinely willed spheres of life with their own laws, which are removed from the Lordship of Jesus Christ, which need not hear his word. It is not a holy sacred part of the world which belongs to Christ, but the whole world.

Now the first question which must be asked is this: *With whose authority does the Church speak when it declares this claim of Christ to the whole world?* With the authority in which alone the Church can speak, with the authority of the Christ living and present in it. The Church is the presence of Christ on earth. . . . For this reason alone its word has authority. The word of the Church is the word of the present Christ, it is Gospel and commandment. It would be the retrogression to the synagogue if its proclamation were commandment alone, and it would be the lapse of the Church into libertinism should it want to deny the commandment of God for the sake of the Gospel. . . . The word of the Church to the world must encounter the world in all its present reality, from the deepest knowledge of the world, if it is to be authoritative. The Church must be able to say the Word of God, the word of authority, here and now, in the most concrete way possible, from knowledge of the situation. The Church may not therefore preach timeless principles, however true, but only commandments which are true today. God is always to us *today*.

How can the Gospel and how can the commandment of the Church be preached with authority, i.e. in quite concrete form? Here lies a problem of the utmost difficulty and magnitude. Can the Church preach the commandment of God with the same certainty with which it preaches the Gospel? Can the Church say 'We need a socialist ordering of the economic system', or 'Do not engage in war', with the same authority as it can say, 'Thy sins be forgiven thee'?

Evidently both Gospel and commandment will only be preached with authority where they are spoken in a quite concrete way. Otherwise things remain in the sphere of what is generally known, human, impotent, false. Where does this principle of concretion lie in the case of the Gospel? Where does it lie in the case of the commandment? This is where the position must be decided. The Gospel becomes concrete in the hearers, the commandment becomes concrete through those who preach it. The phrase 'Thy sins be forgiven thee' is, as the word spoken to the community in proclamation, in the sermon, or in the Eucharist, framed in such a way that it encounters the hearer in completely concrete form. In contrast to this, the commandment needs to be given concrete content by the person who preaches it; the commandment. 'Thou shalt love thy neighbour as thyself' is in itself so general that it needs to be made as concrete as possible if I am to hear what it means for me here and now. And only as a concrete saying is it the Word of God to me. The preacher must therefore be concerned so to incorporate the contemporary situation in his shaping of the commandment that the commandment is itself relevant to the real situation. In the event of taking up a stand about a war, the Church cannot just say, 'There should really be no war, but there are necessary wars' and leave the application of this principle to each individual; it should be able to say quite definitely: 'Engage in this war' or 'Do not engage in this war'. Or in social questions: the last word of the Church should not be to say: 'It is wrong for one man to have too much while another goes hungry, but personal property is God-willed and may not be appropriated', and once again leave the application to the individual. But, if the Church really has a commandment of God, it must proclaim it in the most definite form possible, from the fullest knowledge of the matter, and it must utter a summons to obedience. A commandment must be definite, otherwise it is not a commandment. God's commandment now requires something quite definite from us. And the Church should proclaim this to the community.

But at this point a tremendous difficulty arises. If the Church must know all the details of the situation before it can command, if the validity of its commandment is dependent on its detailed knowledge of a matter, be it war, disarmament, minorities, social questions, the Church always runs the danger of having overlooked this or that relevant point of view in its commandment, or simply of having overestimated it. This again will make the Church completely uncertain in its commandment. Thus the competence of the Church in a matter on which it issues a command is on the one hand a prerequisite for a real commandment, and on the other hand continually makes each of its commandments uncertain, because of this dependence on a complete knowledge of the situation. There are, in principle, two positions which may be adopted in view of the insoluble dilemma: first, there is that of evasion and keeping to general principles. That is the way the churches have almost always gone. Or, alternatively, we can look at the difficulty squarely and then, despite all the dangers, we can venture to do something *either* by keeping a qualified and intentional silence of ignorance *or* by daring to put the commandment definitely, exclusively and radically. In that case the Church will dare to say, 'Do not engage in this war'. 'Now be socialists', uttering this commandment as the commandment of God in the clear recognition that this cannot be so. In so doing the Church will recognize that it is blaspheming the name of God, erring and sinning, but it may speak thus in faith in the promise of the forgiveness of sins, which applies also to the Church. Thus the preaching of the commandment is grounded in the preaching of the forgiveness of sins. The Church cannot command without itself standing in faith in the forgiveness of sins and without indicating this in its preaching of the forgiveness of sins to all those whom it commands. The preaching of the forgiveness of sins is the guarantee of the validity of the preaching of the commandment. Now does this preaching of the forgiveness of sins itself in its turn need a guarantee of its validity? The guarantee of the validity of the preaching of the forgiveness of sins is the sacrament. Here the general saying, 'Thy sins be forgiven thee', is bound up with water, wine and bread, here it comes to be put in all its own distinctness, which is understood as the concrete here and now of the Word of

God only by those who hear it in faith. What the sacrament is for the preaching of the Gospel, the knowledge of firm reality is for the preaching of the sacrament. *Reality is the sacrament of command*. Just as the sacraments of Baptism and Communion are the sole forms of the first reality of creation in this age, and just as they are sacraments, because of this their relation to the original creation, so the 'ethical sacrament' of reality is to be described as a sacrament only in so far as this reality is itself wholly grounded in its relationship to the reality of creation. Thus, just as the fallen world and fallen reality only exist in their relationship to the created world and created reality, so the commandment rests on the forgiveness of sins. The Church preaches the Gospel and the commandment with authority. Now as far as the task which the World Alliance has set itself is concerned we are involved here in the question of giving a definite divine commandment to the world. We saw that this commandment can only be given on the basis of belief in the forgiveness of sins. But it must be given, as long as the world is not the Church.

Whence does the Church know God's commandment for the moment? For it is evidently by no means obvious. 'We know not what to do!' (2 Chronicles 20:12). 'Oh, hide not thy commandments from me!' (Psalm 119:19). The recognition of God's command is an act of God's revelation. Where does the Church receive this revelation? The first answer could be '*The Biblical Law, the Sermon on the Mount* is the absolute norm for our action!' We have simply to take the Sermon on the Mount seriously and to realize it. That is our obedience towards God's commandment. To this we must say: Even the Sermon on the Mount may not become the letter of the law to us. In its commandments it is the demonstration of what God's commandment can be, not what it is, today for us. No one can hear that except ourselves, and God must say it to us today. The commandment is not there once and for all but it is given afresh again and again. Only in this way are we free from the law which interposes itself between us and God; only in this way do we hear God.

The *second answer* would find God's answer in *the orders of creation*. Because certain orders are evident in creation, one should not rebel against them, but simply accept them. One can then argue: Because the nations have been created different, each one is obliged to preserve and develop its characteristics. That is obedience towards the Creator. And if this obedience leads one to struggle and to war, these too must be regarded as belonging to the order of creation. Here too, the commandment of God is thought of as something which has been given once and for all, in definite ordinances which permit of discovery. Now there is a special danger in this argument, and because it is the one most used at the moment, it must be given special attention. The danger of the argument lies in the fact that just about everything can be defended by it. One need only hold out something to be God-willed and God-created for it to be vindicated for ever, the division of man into nations, national struggles, war, class struggle, the exploitation of the weak by the strong, the cut-throat competition of economics. Nothing simpler than to describe all this – because it is there – as God-willed, and therefore to sanction it. But the mistake lies in the fact that in the solution of this apparently so simple equation the great unknown factor is overlooked, the factor which makes this solution impossible. It is not realized in all seriousness that the world is fallen and that now sin prevails, and that creation and sin are so bound up together that no human eye can any longer separate the one from the other, that each human order is an order of the fallen world and not an order of creation. There is no longer any possibility of regarding any features *per se* as orders of creation and of perceiving the will of God *directly* in them. The so-called orders of creation are no longer *per se* revelations of the divine commandment, they are concealed and invisible. Thus the concept of orders of creation must be rejected as a basis for the knowledge of the commandment of God. Hence, neither the Biblical Law as such nor the so-called orders of creation as such are for us the divine commandment which we receive today.

The commandment cannot stem from anywhere but the origin of promise and fulfilment, from Christ. From Christ alone must we know what we should do. But not from him as the preaching prophet of the Sermon on the Mount, but from him as the one who gives us life and forgiveness, as the one who has fulfilled the commandment of God in our place, as the one who brings and promises the new world. We can only perceive the commandment where the law is fulfilled, where the new world of the new order of God is established. Thus we are completely directed towards Christ. Now with this we also understand the whole world order of fallen creation as directed towards Christ, towards the new creation. What has hitherto been dark and obscured from our sight comes into a new light. It is not as though we knew all at once from Jesus Christ what features we should regard as orders of creation, and what not, but that we know that *all* the orders of the world only exist in that they are directed towards Christ: they all stand under the preservation of God as long as they are still open for Christ, they are *orders of preservation*, not orders of creation. They obtain their value solely from outside themselves, from Christ, from the new creation. Their value does not rest in themselves, in other words they are not to be regarded as orders of creation which *per se* are 'very good', but they are God's orders of preservation, which only exist as long as they are open for the revelation of Christ. Preservation is God's act with the fallen world, through which he guarantees the possibility of the new creation. Orders of preservation are forms of working against sin in the direction of the Gospel. Any *order* – however ancient and sacred it may be – *can be dissolved*, and must be dissolved when it closes itself up in itself, grows rigid and no longer permits the proclamation of revelation. From this standpoint the Church of Christ has to pass its verdict on the orders of the world. And it is from this standpoint that the commandment of God must be heard. In the historical change of the orders of the world it has to keep in mind only one thing: Which orders can best restrain this radical falling of the world into death and sin and hold the way open for the Gospel? . . . The commandment of Christ is therefore quite simply the critical and radical commandment, which is limited by nothing else. . . . For the Church to venture a decision for or against an order of preservation would be an impossibility if it did not happen in faith in the God who in Christ forgives even the Church its sins. But in this faith the decision must be ventured.

The churches included in the World Alliance think that they recognize a quite definite order as commanded for us by God today. Today God's commandment for us is the order of *international peace*. To say this is to express a quite definite recognition of the will of God for our time. This recognition should now be analysed and interpreted in the light of what has so far been said. What can the Church say as God's commandment about international peace? So runs the question. First, like anyone who utters God's command, it exposes itself to the suspicion of being fanatical, and of preaching dreams, that is, of speaking from the flesh and not from the spirit. It cannot 'qualify' its word as God's commandment through anything but continued, monotonous, sober reference to this commandment. It will attempt in vain to resist the scandal of pacifist humanitarianism where the commandment of peace is not already itself seen as the commandment of God. The Church must know this and resist any attempt at a justification of God's commandment. It gives the commandment, but no more.

Under the predominant influence of Anglo-Saxon theological thought in the World Alliance, the peace envisaged here has been previously understood as the reality of the Gospel, we may almost say, as part of the kingdom of God on earth. From this standpoint the ideal of peace is made absolute, i.e. it is no longer regarded as something expedient, as an order of preservation, but as a final order of perfection, valid in itself, as the penetration of another order into the fallen world. External peace is a 'very good' condition in itself. It is thus an order of creation and of the kingdom of God, and as such must be preserved unconditionally. But this conception must be repudiated as unbalanced, and therefore untrue to the Gospel. International peace is not a reality of the Gospel, not a part of the kingdom of God, but a command of the angry God, an order for the preservation of the world in the light of Christ. International peace is therefore no ideal state, but an order which is directed towards something else and not valid in itself. The making of such an order of preservation can of course become a matter of absolute urgency, but never for its own sake; it is mainly for the sake of him towards whom it is directed, namely for the sake of the receiver of the revelation. The broken character of the order of peace is expressed in the fact that the peace demanded by God has two limits, first the truth and secondly justice. There can only be a community of peace when it does not rely on *lies* and on *injustice*. Where a community of peace endangers or chokes truth and justice, the community of peace must be broken and battle joined. If the battle is then on both sides really waged for truth and for justice, the community of peace, though outwardly destroyed, is made all the deeper and stronger in the battle over this same cause. But should it become clear that one of the combatants is only fighting for his own selfish ends, should even this form of the community of peace be broken, there is revealed that reality which is the ultimate and only tolerable ground of any community of peace, the forgiveness of sins. There is a community of peace for Christians only because one will forgive the other his sins. The forgiveness of sins still remains the sole ground of all peace, even where the order of eternal peace remains preserved in truth and justice. It is therefore also the ultimate ground on which all ecumenical work rests, precisely where the cleavage appears hopeless. . . .

If the ordering of eternal peace is not timelessly valid, but penetrable at any time, simply because the complete expression of the truth and justice would threaten to make the hearing of the revelation in Christ impossible, then *struggle* is made comprehensible in principle, as a possibility of action in the light of Christ. Struggle is not an order of creation, but it can be an order of preservation for Christ's new creation. Struggle can in some cases guarantee openness for the revelation in Christ better than external peace, in that it breaks apart the hardened self-enclosed order.

There is, however, a very widespread extremely dangerous error about today that the *justification* of *struggle* already contains the justification of war, affirms war in principle. The right of war can be derived from the right of struggle as little as the use of torture may be derived from the necessity of legal procedures in human society. Anyone who has seriously studied the history of the concept of war from Luther to Fichte and Bismarck and then on to the present, knows that while the word has remained the same, its content has become something absolutely incomparable. War in our day no longer falls under the concept of struggle because it is the certain self-annihilation of both combatants. It is in no way to be regarded as an order of preservation in the light of revelation, simply because it is so destructive. The power of annihilation extends both to the inner and the outer man. War today destroys both soul and body. Now because we can in no way understand war as one of God's orders of preservation, and thus as the commandment of God, and because on the other hand war needs idealizing and idolizing to be able to live, war today, and therefore the next war, must be utterly *rejected* by the Church. . . . Not from the fanatical erection of one commandment – perhaps the sixth – over the others, but from obedience towards the commandment of God which is directed towards us today, that war shall be no more because it takes away the possibility of seeing revelation. Nor should we be afraid of the word 'pacificism' today. As certainly as we leave the making of the last peace to God, so certainly should we also make peace to overcome war. It is obvious that struggle as such will not be driven out of the world in this way. But here we are concerned with a quite definite means of struggle which today stands under God's prohibition. . . .

The will of God is directed not only to the new creating of men, but also to the new creating of conditions. It is wrong to say that only the will can be good. Conditions too can be good. God's creation was *per se* 'very good'. Conditions can be good even in the fallen world, but never in themselves, and always only in the light of the action of God for his new creation. We cannot restore the creation, but under God's commandment we should create such conditions – and here we have all the hardness of the divine commandment – as are good in respect of what the God who commands today will himself do, in respect of the new creation by Christ. Conditions are good only 'in respect of' something else. But in this they are good, and as such, the peace which overcomes war is 'good'.

Now the World Alliance thinks that it can guarantee this peace by working for 'understanding'. We would ask: How is such *understanding* conceivable and obtainable *in a Christian way*? The original, Anglo-Saxon view of the World Alliance, without doubt still prevailing today, is 'Understanding by personal acquaintance'. Indispensible as this first step is, it is by no means the only one or the most important one. Socialism has succeeded in setting itself up on an international basis not because the German worker knows the French and the English worker, but because they have a common ideal. Similarly, Christians too will only learn to think internationally when they have a great, common message. We need today more than anything else in the ecumenical movement the one great reconciling message. Let us not deceive ourselves, we do not have this message yet. The language of the ecumenical movement is – in spite of everything – weak. But this message will only come together with a theology. Thus here, at the end, we are led back to our first concern. Understanding in the best and truest sense comes only through present preaching and theology. There is such a tremendous danger that at international conferences we shall find friendship, 'good fellowship' with one another, and nothing else. But 'even the heathen and the tax-gatherers do that'. We are concerned with something else, with a new knowledge and a new will. And where each conference does not move towards this goal with the utmost seriousness, time is lost and gossiped away. And anyone who has been to international conferences with this aim will know that it demands hard work and a hard struggle. But that is what such conferences are for.

[*Address at the Youth Peace Conference in Czechoslovakia, 26 July 1932*][1]

6

A VOICE FOR THE JEWS

THE CHURCH AND THE JEWISH QUESTION

Luther 1546: 'We would still show them the Christian doctrine and ask them to return and accept the Lord whom they should by rights have honoured before we did' . . . 'Where they repent, leave their usury, and accept Christ, we would gladly regard them as our brothers.'

Luther 1523: 'If the Apostles, who also were Jews, had dealt with the Gentiles as we Gentiles deal with the Jews, there would have been no Christians among the Gentiles. But seeing that they have acted in such a brotherly way towards us, we in turn should act in a brotherly way towards the Jews in case we might convert some. For we ourselves are not fully their equals, much less their superiors . . . But now we use force against them . . . what good will we do them with that? Similarly, how will we benefit them by forbidding them to live and work and have other human fellowship with us, thus driving them to practise usury?'

The fact, unique in history, that the Jew has been made subject to special laws by the state solely because of the race to which he belongs, and quite apart from his religious beliefs, raises two new problems for the theologian, which must be examined separately. What is the Church's attitude to this action by the state? And what should the Church do as a result of it? That is one question. The other is, what attitude should the Church take to its members who are baptized Jews? Both questions can only be answered in the light of a true concept of the Church.

1

Without doubt the Church of the Reformation has no right to address the state directly in its specifically practical actions. It has neither to praise nor to censure the laws of the state, but must rather affirm the state to be God's order of preservation in a godless world; it has to recognize the state's ordinances, good or bad as they appear from a humanitarian point of view, and to understand that they are based on the sustaining will of God amidst the chaotic godlessness of the world. This view of the state's action on the part of the Church is far removed beyond any form of moralism and is distinct from humanitarianism of any shade through the radical nature of the gulf between the standpoint of the Gospel and the standpoint of the Law. The action of the state remains free from the Church's intervention. There are no piqued or pedantic comments from the Church here. History is made not by the Church but by the state; but of course only the Church, which bears witness to the coming of God in history, knows what history and therefore what the state is. And precisely because of this knowledge, it alone testifies to the penetration of history by God in Christ and lets the state continue to make history. Without doubt the Jewish question is one of the historical problems which our state must deal with, and without doubt the state is justified in adopting new methods here. It remains the concern of humanitarian associations, and individual Christians who feel themselves called to the task, to remind the state of the moral side of any of its measures, i.e. on occasions to accuse the state of offences against morality. Any strong state needs such associations and such individuals, and will to some extent take good care of them. It is an insight into the finer arts of statesmanship which knows how to make use of these spokesmen in their relative significance. In the same way, a Church which is essentially regarded as a cultural function of the state must at times contact the state with such reminders, and must do so all the more strongly as the state takes the Church to itself, i.e. ascribes to it essentially moral and pedagogic tasks.

The true Church of Christ, however, lives solely from the Gospel and realizes the character of the state's actions, and will never intervene in the state in such a way as to criticize its history-making actions, from the standpoint of some humanitarian ideal. It recognizes the absolute necessity of the use of force in this world and also the 'moral' injustice of certain acts of the state which are necessarily bound up with the use of force. The Church cannot in the first place exert direct political action, for the Church does not pretend to have any knowledge of the necessary course of history. Thus, even today, in the Jewish question, it cannot address the state directly and demand of it some definite action of a different nature. But that does not mean that it lets political action slip by disinterestedly; it can and should, precisely because it does not moralize in individual instances, continually ask the state, i.e. as action which leads to law and order, and not to lawlessness and disorder. It is called to put this question with great emphasis where the state appears to be threatened precisely in its nature as the state whether its action can be justified as legitimate action of the state, i.e. in its function of creating law and order by means of force. It will have to put this question quite clearly today in the matter of the Jewish question. In so doing, it does not encroach on the state's sphere of responsibility but on the contrary fathers upon the state itself the whole weight of the responsibility for its own particular actions. In this way it frees the state from any charge of moralizing and shows precisely thus its appointed function as the preserver of the world. As long as the state continues to create law and order by its acts, even if it be a new law and a new order, the Church of the Creator, the Mediator and the Redeemer cannot engage in direct political action against it. It may not of course prevent the individual Christian, who knows himself called to the task, from calling the state 'inhuman' on occasions, but *qua* church it will only ask whether the state is bringing about law and order or not.

Now here, of course, the state sees itself to be limited in two respects. Both too much law and order and too little law and order compel the Church to speak. There is too little law and order where a group of men becomes lawless, though in real life it is sometimes extraordinarily difficult to distinguish real lawlessness from a formally permitted minimum of law. Even in slavery a minimum of law and order was preserved, and yet a reintroduction of slavery would mean real lawlessness. It is nevertheless worth noting that Christian churches tolerated slavery for eighteen centuries, and that a new law was made only at a time when the Christian substance of the Church could at least be put in question, with the help of the churches (but not essentially or even solely by them). However, to the Church a step back in this direction would be the expression of a lawless state. It follows that the concept of law is subject to historical change, and this in its turn once again confirms the state in its characteristic history-making law. It is not the Church, but the state, which makes and changes the law.

Too little law and order stands in contrast to too much law and order. That means that the state develops its power to such an extent that it deprives Christian preaching and Christian faith (not freedom of conscience — that would be the humanitarian illusion, which is illusory because my life in a state constrains the so-called 'free conscience') of their rights — a grotesque situation, as the state only receives its peculiar rights from this proclamation and from this faith, and enthrones itself by means of them. The Church must reject the encroachment of the order of the state precisely because of its better knowledge of the state and of the limitations of its action. The state which endangers Christian proclamation negates itself.

All this means is that there are three possible ways in which the Church can act towards the state: in the first place, as has been said, it can ask the state whether its actions are legitimate and in accordance with its character as state, i.e. it can throw the state back upon its responsibilities. Secondly, it can aid the victims of state action. The Church has an unconditional obligation to the victims of any ordering of society, even if they do not belong to the Christian community. 'Do good to all men.' In both these courses of action, the Church serves the free state in its free way, and at times when laws are changed the Church in no way withdraws itself from these two tasks. The third possibility is not just to bandage the victims under the wheel, but to put a spoke in the wheel itself. Such action would be direct political action, and is only possible and demanded when the Church sees the state fail in its function of creating law and order, i.e. when it sees the state unrestrainedly bring about too much or too little law and order . . . There would be too little law if any group of subjects were deprived of their rights, too much when the state intervened in the character of the Church and its proclamation, e.g. in the forced exclusion of baptized Jews from our Christian congregations or in the prohibition of our mission to the Jews. Here the Christian Church would find itself in *statu confessionis* and here the state would be in the act of negating itself. A state which includes within itself a terrorized Church has lost its most faithful servant. But even the third action of the Church, which on occasion leads to conflict with the existing state, is only the paradoxical expression of its ultimate recognition of the state: indeed, the Church itself knows itself to be called here to protect the state *qua* state from itself and preserve it. In the Jewish problem the first two possibilities will be the compelling demands of the hour. The necessity of direct political action by the church is, on the other hand, to be decided at any time by an 'Evangelical Council' and cannot therefore be casuistically decided beforehand.

Now the measures of the state towards Judaism stands in a quite special context for the Church. The Church of Christ has never lost sight of the thought that the 'chosen people', who nailed the redeemer of the world to the cross, must bear the curse for its action through a long history of suffering.

> Jews are the poorest people among all nations upon earth,
> they are tossed to and fro, they are scattered here and
> there in all lands, they have no certain place where they
> may remain safely and must always be afraid that they
> will be driven out (Luther's *Table Talk*).

But the history of the suffering of this people, loved and punished by

God, stands under the sign of the final home-coming of the people of Israel to its God. And this home-coming happens in the conversion of Israel to Christ.

> When the time comes that this people humbles itself and penitently departs from the sins of its fathers to which it has clung with fearful stubbornness to this day, and calls down upon itself the blood of the Crucified One for reconciliation, then the world will wonder at the miracle that God works, that he works with his people! And then the overweening Philistines will be like dung in the streets and chaff on the rooftops. Then he will gather this people from all nations and bring it back to Canaan. O Israel, who is like thee? Happy the people whose God is the Lord!
> (S. Menken, 1795)

The conversion of Israel, that is to be the end of the people's suffering. From here the Christian Church sees the history of the people of Israel with trembling as God's own, free, fearful way with his people. It knows that no nation in the world can be finished with this mysterious people, because God is not yet finished with it. Each new attempt to 'solve the Jewish problem' comes to nothing on the saving-historical significance of this people; nevertheless, such attempts must continually be made. This consciousness on the part of the Church of the curse that bears down upon this people, raises it far above any cheap moralizing; instead, as it looks at the rejected people, it humbly recognizes itself as a church continually unfaithful to its Lord and looks full of hope to those of the people of Israel who have come home, to those who have come to believe in the one true God in Christ, and knows itself to be bound to them in brotherhood.

2

The Church cannot allow its actions towards its members to be prescribed by the state. The baptized Jew is a member of our

Church. Thus the Jewish problem is not the same for the Church as it is for the state.

From the point of view of the Church of Christ, Judaism is never a racial concept but a religious one. What is meant is not the biologically questionable entity of the Jewish race, but the 'people of Israel'. Now the 'people' of Israel is constituted by the law of God; a man can thus become a Jew by taking the Law upon himself. But no one can become a Jew by race. In the time of the great Jewish mission to the Gentile world there were different stages of membership of Judaism. In the same way, the concept of Jewish Christianity has religious, not biological content. The Jewish-Christian mission also stretched to Gentile territory (Paul's opponents in Galatians). There were Gentile Jewish-Christians and Jewish Gentile-Christians.

Thus from the point of view of the Church it is not baptized Christians of Jewish race who are Jewish Christians; in the Church's views the Jewish Christian is the man who lets membership of the people of God, of the Church of Christ, be determined by the observance of a divine law. In contrast the Gentile Christian knows no presupposition for membership of the people of God, the Church of Christ, but the call of God by his Word in Christ.

There would be an analogous situation today where a church group within the Reformation Church allowed membership of the Church to be determined by the observance of a divine law; for example, the racial unity of the members of the community. The Jewish-Christian type materializes where this demand is put irrespectively of whether its proponents belong to the Jewish race or not. Then there is the further possibility that the modern Jewish-Christian type withdraws from the Gentile-Christian community and founds its own church community based on the law. But it is in that case impossible for church to exclude from the community that part of the community which belongs to the Jewish race because it destroys the legalistic, Jewish Christian claim. For that would be to demand that the Gentile-Christian community be made Jewish-Christian, and that is a claim which it must rightly refuse.

The exclusion of Jews by race from our German church would bring this latter into the Jewish-Christian category. Such an exclusion thus remains impossible for the Church.

There is nothing to hinder a voluntary association of Christians of Jewish race in one church; but the forced expulsion of Gentile-Christian Jews from Gentile-Christian congregations of German race is in no case permissible, quite apart from the difficulty of demonstrating that these Jews are not Germans. Such a forced ejection — even if it did not have a corporate, organized character — would still represent a real split in the Church, simply because it would raise the racial unity of the Church to the status of a law which would have to be fulfilled as a presupposition for church membership. In doing this the church community which did the excluding would constitute itself a Jewish-Christian community.

It was this difference in the understanding of the appearance of Christ and of the Gospel alone which led to the first division of the Church of Christ and it was regarded on both sides partly as intolerable heresy and partly as intolerable schism. What is at stake is by no means the question of whether our German members can still tolerate church fellowship with the Jews. It is rather the task of Christian preaching to say: here is the Church, where Jew and German stand together under the Word of God; here is the proof whether the Church is still the Church or not. No one who feels unable to tolerate church fellowship with Christians of Jewish race can be prevented from separating himself from this church fellowship. But it must then be made clear to him with the utmost seriousness that he is thus loosing himself from the place on which the Church of Christ stands, and that he is thus bringing to reality the Jewish-Christian idea of a religion based on law, i.e. is falling into modern Jewish-Christianity. One must have an extraordinarily restricted view not to see that any attitude of our church towards the baptized Jews among our people, other than that described above, would meet with widespread misunderstanding.

Luther on Psalm 110:3: 'There is no other rule or test for who is a member of the people of God or the Church of Christ than this: where there is a little band of those who accept this word of the Lord, teach it purely and confess against those who persecute it, and for that reason suffer what is their due.

[*An article written on 7 May 1933, in protest against the Aryan Clause promulgated on 7 April, depriving those of Jewish origin (however remote) from holding office in the state and church.*][1]

BARTH AND THE ARYAN CLAUSE

Bonhoeffer to Barth (9 September 1933): In your booklet (*Theological Existence Today,* No 1) you said that where a church adopted the Aryan Clause it would cease to be a Christian church. A considerable number of pastors here would agree with you in this view. Now the expected has happened, and I am therefore asking you on behalf of many friends, pastors and students, to let us know whether you feel that it is possible either to remain in a church which has ceased to be a Christian church or to continue to exercise a ministry which has become a privilege for Aryans. We have in the first place drawn up a declaration in which we wish to inform the church authorities that, with the Aryan Clause, the Evangelical Church of the Old Prussian Union has cut itself off from the Church of Christ. We want to wait for the answer to it, i.e. to see whether the signatories will be dismissed from their posts or whether they will be allowed to say something of this sort unmolested. Several of us are now very drawn to the idea of a Free Church. The difference between our present situation and that of Luther lies in the fact that the Catholic Church expelled Luther under its laws against heresy, while our church authorities can do nothing of the sort because they completely lack any concept of heresy. It is therefore by no means simple to argue from Luther's attitude. I know that many people now wait on your judgement; I also know that most of them are of the opinion that you will counsel us to wait until we are thrown out. In fact, however, there are people who have already been thrown out, i.e. the Jewish Christians, and the same thing will very soon happen to others on grounds which have absolutely no connection with the Church. What is the consequence for us if the Church really is not just an individual congregation in any one place? How do things stand with the solidarity of the pastorate? When is there any possibility of leaving the Church? There can be no doubt at all that the *status confessionis* has arrived; what we are by no means clear about is how the *confessio* is most appropriately expressed today.

[*Letter sent with a copy of a 'draft of a confession of faith' which Bonhoeffer helped to write*][2]

DECLARATION

According to the confession of our church, the teaching office of the church is bound up with a call to the ministry of the church and with that call alone. The 'Aryan Clause' of the new enactment concerning offices in the church puts forward a principle which contradicts this basic clause of the confession. As a result, a position which must be regarded as unjust is proclaimed as church law, and the confession is violated.

There can be no doubt that as long as the ordained ministers affected by the enactment are not dispossessed of the rights which belong to their status as ministers by formal proceedings, they have under all circumstances the right to preach the Word and administer the sacraments freely in the Evangelical Church of the Old Prussian Union which rests on the confessions of the Reformation.

Anyone who gives his assent to a breach of the confession thereby excludes himself from the community of the Church. We therefore demand that this law, which separates the Evangelical Church of the Old Prussian Union from the Christian Church, be repealed forthwith.

7 September 1933
Martin Niemöller
Dietrich Bonhoeffer

[*The declaration referred to in the letter to Barth, which became the draft for a call to the ministers to form the Pastors' Emergency League*][3]

7

PASTORATES IN ENGLAND
1933-1935

ADDRESS TO THE NATIONAL CHURCH
GOVERNMENT IN BERLIN

Bradford, 29 November 1933: The German Evangelical pastors today assembled in Bradford for their Pastors' Conference note with pleasure and satisfaction that in his declaration of 14 November 1933 the National Bishop stood out firmly for purity of doctrine.

Despite this declaration, the most recent decisions of the Church, the most recent developments within the 'German Christian Movement', and public and private statements on the occasion of the visit of prominent church leaders in England, lead us to make a declaration to which we have been driven by great concern for the future of the Church and of our congregations.

1. We hope and expect of all who bear office in the church and in the church government that in accordance with the pledge of the National Bishop, they acknowledge in word and deed the doctrine of faith in the grace of Jesus Christ which alone brings justification — the sole basis of Reformation thought — as the teaching of the Church, and that all possible care will be taken that all who hold office present this basic position to strangers and outsiders also, and maintain it above all doubt in the future.

2. We hope and expect that the formal principle of the German Reformation — that the Holy Scriptures of the New and Old Testaments are the sole norm of faith — remain absolutely intact in every respect. Confidence in the leadership of the Church threatens

to be seriously damaged when members of church governments severely jeopardize the force of this Reformation principle by their, to us, incomprehensible public conduct or lend their support to such movements as seek to destroy the inalienable heritage of the German Reformation.

We would point out that any doubt in the inviolability of the material and formal principles of the Reformation must result in serious disruption in the church life of the German Evangelical congregations in Great Britain, and must inevitably break the close connection between the German Evangelical diaspora in England and the church at home.

Revolted and ashamed at the attacks on the substance of Evangelical faith in Luther's Year 1933, and on the occasion of the enthronement of the National Bishop, for the sake of the unity and purity of the Church we express our hope and expectation that the German Evangelical Church will always continue to remain the Church of the Reformation.

[*This address to the Church Government, with a similar one to the President of Germany, was signed by six pastors of German-speaking congregations in England, including Bonhoeffer, who initiated the move and drafted the 'address'.*]

CORRESPONDENCE TO THE BISHOP OF CHICHESTER

27 December 1933: It means very much to me to know that you are sharing the sorrows and the troubles which the last year has brought to our church in Germany. So we do not stand alone and whatever may occur to one member of the Church universal, we know that all the members suffer with it. Things in Germany are going on more slowly than we expected. Müller's position (the National Bishop) is, of course, very much endangered. But he seems to try to find closer contact with the state to be sure of its protection in case of danger. Only from this point of view can I understand his last agreement with the Hitler Youth (more or less handing over the Church's youth work to the Hitler Youth). But it seems as if the state is, nevertheless, very much reserved and does not want to interfere once more. I do not think personally that Müller can keep his position, and it will certainly be a great success if he falls. But we must not think that the fight is settled then. On the contrary, it will without any doubt start anew and probably sharper than before, with the only advantage that the fronts have been cleared. The trend towards nordic heathenism is growing tremendously, particularly among very influential circles; and I am afraid the opposition is not united in their aims. In Berlin they are going to form an Emergency Synod under the leadership of Jacobi next Friday. This is meant to be a legal representation of the oppositional congregations against the illegal synods of last August and September. Jacobi is probably the wisest of the oppositional leaders at the moment and I put much trust in what he is doing. There is a great danger that people who have had a very indifferent attitude towards the German Christians last summer, jeopardize now the success of the opposition by mingling in and seeking their own personal advantage.

The letter of Müller, as expected, was very weak and anxious, it really does not mean anything at all. It does not come out of a sound theological, but much more of a political argumentation. If you allow me, I shall be only too glad to come to Chichester again. I am still having continuous information by telephone and airmail from Berlin.

14 March 1934: May I just let you know that I was called last week again to Berlin — this time by the church government. The subject was the ecumenic situation. I also saw Niemöller, Jacobi and some friends from the Rhineland. The Free Synod (i.e. of the Confessing Church) was a real progress and success. We hope to get ready for a Free National Synod, 18 April in Barmen. One of the most important things is that the Christian churches of the other countries do not lose their interest in the conflict by the length of time. I know that my friends are looking to you and your further actions with great hope. There is really a moment now as perhaps never before in Germany in which our faith in the ecumenic tasks of the churches can be shaken and destroyed completely or strengthened and renewed in a surprisingly new way. And it is you, my Lord Bishop, on whom it depends whether this moment will be used. The question at stake in the German church is no longer an internal issue, but is the question of existence of Christianity in Europe; therefore a definite attitude of the ecumenic movement has nothing to do with 'intervention' — it is just a demonstration to the whole world that Church and Christianity as such are at stake. Even if the information in the newspapers is becoming less interesting, the real situation is as tense, as acute, as responsible as ever. Please do not be silent now! I beg you once more to consider the possibility of an ecumenic delegation and ultimatum . . . in the name of Christianity in Europe. Time passes by very quickly, and it might soon be too late. May Day will be declared by Müller, 'Peace in the Church' day. Six weeks only.

15 April 1934: It is on the urgent request of one of my German friends, whose name I would rather mention to you personally, that I am writing to you again. I have received yesterday this letter which has upset me very much indeed, and I think it is necessary that you know how our friends in Germany are feeling, about the present situation and about the task of the ecumenic movement. The letter is really an outcry against the latest events in the German church, and a last appeal for an 'unmisunderstandable' word of the ecumenic movement. This man, who speaks for a few thousand others, states quite frankly: 'In the present moment there depends everything, absolutely everything, on the attitude of the Bishop of Chichester.' This means that the moment has definitely come for a definite attitude — perhaps in the way of an ultimatum or in expressing publicly sympathy with the oppositional pastors; or to lose all confidence in the ecumenic movement among the best elements of the German pastors, an outlook which terrifies me . . . Of course, pastors in Germany do not realize all the implications which are connected with such a step taken by the ecumenic movement, but they certainly have a very fine feeling for the right spiritual moment for the churches abroad to speak their word . . . As to the facts, there is firstly the appointment of Dr Jäger, which is considered to be an ostentatious affront to the opposition, and which means in fact that all power in the church government has been handed over to political and party authorities. It was much surprising to me that *The Times* gave a rather positive report about this appointment. Dr Jäger is the man who said that Jesus was only the exponent of a nordic religion for a nordic race. He was the man who caused the retirement of Bodelschwingh (the first national bishop elected, before Müller) and who was considered to be the most ruthless man in church government. Furthermore, he is, and remains, the head of the church department in the Prussian Ministry of Education and a leading member of the party. So this appointment must be taken as a significant step towards the complete assimilation of the Church to the state and party. Even if Jäger should try to make himself (appear) sympathetic to the churches abroad by using mild words now, one must not be deceived by this tactic.

29 June 1934 (commenting on a letter from Dr Fabricius, which the Bishop had sent on to him for such comment):
Dr Fabricius is an Assistant Professor in the University of Berlin. He is considered to be ill and much embittered. His influence among the younger generation and his theological significance have always been limited . . . I heartily disapprove of the whole tone and tenor of his letter . . . After a long talk with Dr Winterhager, I should like to submit to you the following points as possibly forming the outline to the answer, however shortly any answer should be: Dr Fabricius maintains that there is a large difference between the official German Christians and the 'German Faith Movement'. In fact this difference is extremely small! We may prove this by three statements:

1. Dr Krause's party, affiliated to the German Faith Movement, is still officially within the church 'communion' and is entitled to send its representatives to both parish councils and governing bodies.

2. An 'ecclesiastic member' of the German Faith Movement (a curate) has recently (at an open meeting attended by Dr Coch-Dresden, Bishop of Sachsen) read the following passage from the Gospel according to St John: 'In the beginning was the Nation, and the Nation was with God, and the Nation was God, and the same was in the beginning with God, etc.' Bishop Coch did not express one word of disagreement with this new version of the New Testament. Several ministers of the Opposition who witnessed this event wrote to Bishop Müller and asked him to correct this reading. Nothing was done.

3. The President of Brandenburg, Herr Kube, Member of the General Synod of the (official) church in Prussia, and one of the responsible leaders of the German Christians, concluded his latest Midsummer-Night speech by saying; 'Adolf Hitler yesterday, today and forever'.

Dr Fabricius . . . asks for information to what extent the German Evangelical Church can be said to be in danger 'to cease to be Christian' . . . The points which you, my Lord Bishop, make in your letter today are all based on facts which make it doubtful whether the German church has not already ceased to be a Christian church — the Aryan Clause, unreserved homage demanded for the state, the use of force, prohibition of free elections (i.e. church elections), the introduction of the leadership principle with the autocratic powers given to Bishop Müller.

24 October 1934: . . . I could imagine Hitler saying that he would not interfere in the church conflict, nor even in the situation of schism. He would leave it all to the church and, of course, in fact leave it to some 'Nazi' groups to interfere on their own initiative and so terrorize the true Evangelical Church in Germany. I have been thinking much more about your question, what Hitler could do in case he was willing to settle the conflict. From his point of view I can only see the one way of dismissing Jäger and Müller and nominating a representative of the Opposition — possibly a lawyer, not a theologian, Dr Flor of the *Reichsgericht* (national court) — with the special task to restitute legal and confessional conditions in the church. After a certain period of vacancy a new *Reichsbishop* (national Bishop) might be elected by a legal National Synod. This interim, however, should last for at least one year, so that the general excitement may have passed. There is a certain difficulty if Hitler nominates a theologian who would become *Reichsbishof* afterwards. We have always disapproved of the nomination of Müller, not only personally, but also fundamentally. Hitler may nominate a lawyer, but he just wants to confirm a theologian. The fact that Hitler has consulted the Reichsminister Gürtner (of Justice) last Saturday perhaps indicates a move in the right direction.

THE CHURCH AND THE PEOPLES OF THE WORLD

'I will hear what God the Lord will speak: for he will speak peace unto his people, and to his saints' (Psalm 85:8).

Between the twin crags of nationalism and internationalism ecumenical Christendom calls upon her Lord and asks his guidance. Nationalism and internationalism have to do with political possibilities and necessities. The ecumenical church, however, does not concern itself with these things, but with the commandments of God, and, regardless of circumstances, it transmits these commandments to the world.

Our task, as theologians, accordingly consists only in accepting this commandment as a binding one, not as a question open to discussion. Peace on earth is not a problem, but a commandment given at Christ's coming. There are two ways of reacting to this commandment from God: the unconditional, blind obedience of action, or the hypocritical question of the Serpent: 'Yea, hath God said . . ?' This question is the moral enemy of obedience, and therefore the moral enemy of all real peace. 'Hath God not said? Has God not understood nature well enough to know that wars must occur in the world, like laws of nature? Must God not have meant that we should talk about peace, to be sure, but that it is not to be literally translated into action? Must God not really have said that we should work for peace, of course, but also make ready tanks and poison gas for security? And then perhaps the most serious question: 'Did God say you should not protect your own people? Did God say you should leave your own a prey to the enemy?'

No, God did not say all that. What he has said is that there should be peace among men — that we shall obey him without further question, that is what he means. He who questions the commandments of God before obeying has already denied him.

There shall be peace because of the Church of Christ, for the sake of which the world exists. And this Church of Christ lives at one and the same time in all peoples, yet beyond all boundaries, whether national, political, social or racial. And the brothers who make up the Church are bound together, through the commandment of the one Lord Christ, whose Word they hear, more inseparably than men are bound by all the ties of common history, of blood, of class and of language. All these ties, which are part of our world, are valid ties; but in the presence of Christ they are not ultimate bonds. For the members of the ecumenical church, in so far as they hold to Christ, his word, his commandment of peace is more holy, more inviolable than the most revered words and works of the natural world. For they know that whosoever is not able to hate father and mother for his sake is not worthy of him, and lies if he calls himself after Christ's name. These brothers in Christ obey his word; they do not doubt or question, but keep his commandment of peace. They are not ashamed, in defiance of the world, even to speak of eternal peace. They cannot take up arms against Christ himself - yet this is what they do if they take up arms against one another! Even in anguish and distress of conscience there is for them no escape from the commandment of Christ, for there shall be peace. How does peace come about? Through a system of political treaties? Through the investment of international capital in different countries? Through the big banks, through money? Or through universal peaceful rearmament in order to guarantee peace? Through none of these, for the single reason that in all of them peace is confused with safety. There is no way to peace along the way of safety. For peace must be dared. It is the great venture. It can never be safe. Peace is the opposite of security. To demand guarantees is to mistrust, and this mistrust in turn brings forth war. To look for guarantees is to want to protect oneself. Peace means to give oneself altogether to the law of God, wanting no security, but in faith and obedience laying the destiny of the nations in the hand of Almighty God, not trying to direct it for selfish purposes. Battles are won, not with weapons, but with God. They are won where the way leads to the cross. Which of us can say what it might mean for the world if one nation should meet the aggressor not with weapons in hand, but praying, defenceless, and for that very reason protected by a 'bulwark never failing'?

Once again, how will peace come? Who will call us to peace so that the world will hear, will have to hear, so that all people may rejoice? The individual Christian cannot do it. When all around are silent, he can indeed raise his voice and bear witness, but the powers of the world stride over him without a word. The individual church, too, can witness and suffer — oh, if it only would! — but it also is suffocated by the power of hate. Only the one great Ecumenical Council of the holy Church of Christ over all the world can speak out so that the world, though it gnash its teeth, will have to hear, so that the people will rejoice because the Church of Christ in the name of Christ has taken the weapons from the hands of their sons, forbidden war, proclaimed the peace of Christ against the raging world.

Why do we fear the fury of the world powers? Why don't we take the power from them and give it back to Christ? We can still do it today. The Ecumenical Council is in session; it can send out to all believers this radical call to peace. The nations are waiting for it in the East and in the West. Must we be put to shame by non-Christian people in the East? Shall we desert the individuals who are risking their lives for this message? The hour is late. The world is choked with weapons, and dreadful is the distrust which looks out of all men's eyes. The trumpets of war may blow tomorrow. For what are we waiting? Do we want to become involved in this guilt as never before?

What use to me are crown, land, folk and fame
They cannot cheer my breast.
War's in the land, alas, and on my name
I pray no guilt may rest.   (M. Claudius)

We want to give the world a whole word, not a half word — a courageous word, a Christian word. We want to pray that this word may be
given today. Who knows if we shall see each other again another year.
[*Bonhoeffer's sermon at morning prayers, 28 August 1934, during the
'Life and Work' conference held on the Danish island of Fanö.
Bonhoeffer was recalled to Germany to undertake the theological education of pastors for the Confessing Church.*][3]

8

PREACHERS' SEMINARY, FINKENWALDE, 1935-1937

IN DEFENCE OF THE BEHAVIOUR OF HIS STUDENTS

Finkenwalde, 25 January 1936
Dear Brother S.,
On the meeting at Bredow; I agree with you in feeling that such responsible discussions are only possible if considerable internal and external discipline is preserved. I therefore welcomed the request of the Council of Brethren that there should be no indications of approval. You accuse the brethren of the seminary of not having complied with this request. To this I would reply that our brethren, with the exception of one who was extremely worried about it afterwards, took no part in the shouts of applause at the end of P. Helbig's speech. On the contrary, these methods were most strongly condemned by our brethren. Young and older theologians who sat near us joined in them. I consider it to be extremely important that we should not become confused here. I also know that our brethren tried again and again to keep them quiet. You say that they showed their approval after I had spoken, but only hesitantly after Brother Krause had spoken. It is certainly inappropriate to speak here of 'unrestrained applause' and 'demonic fanaticism'. I am writing this in such detail because I feel it is a bad thing, which really offends against brotherly love, that because of the 'radical attitude' of the Finkenwalde seminary it should now have a reputation for all this sort of thing. In other words, not for the sake of my personal reputation, but because of the common concern for sincerity, brotherliness and right dealing in the church struggle which moves us all. Now I certainly do not want to give the impression that your words do not

apply to us at all. Of course, they apply to us, and how far we know better than anyone else. We had another serious discussion about it only last Monday evening. You know something about our seminary, and I would most sincerely ask you to give us brotherly help and to stand by us in our efforts.

I would ask you to imagine the situation as it must have appeared, especially to the younger brethren. Think of the damning, the irresponsible, the unChristian, the damaging things that were said there. If at a time like that, when the right way or the wrong way for the Church, truth or untruth, was at stake, a time when at every moment there was a danger that the Church might be led fearfully astray, if at a time like that there should for once have been some slight 'psychical' explosion, well I cannot get all that worked up about it. There is something more important that really matters. That is that the truth of the Word of God alone should prevail. Lapses in the tone of speeches and in disciplined conduct can be made good. I know that each of my brothers here is ready to ask pardon for such a lapse. It is much, much harder to make amends, however, if the Church leaves the way of faithfulness and truth in its testimony to Christ. A discipline which no longer leaves room for a passionate protest against the falsification of the truth, no longer stems from a wholeness of obedience to Jesus Christ. It becomes an arbitrary Christian ideal, a self-selected work. I need not tell you that I am one with you in feeling that any indiscipline makes the truth we proclaim impossible to believe. But the promise is held only by the right testimony to Christ and not by the work of discipline.

Brother Krause's speech did not strike me as very good either. I could not regard it as a clear testimony. However, after Brother Krause told me that you had said that Satan spoke through him, I began to take his side. I can only regard your verdict as being uncharitable, showing a vindictiveness which disquietens me far more than the vindictiveness that you condemn in our theological approach. About Brother Krause, he did not say that Marahrens was a traitor, but that he had betrayed the Church, which is quite different. The latter is a judgement on an objective decision and action, and not on a person. It is possible to dispute the theological justification of this statement, but my only objection to it would be that Marahrens could not have betrayed the Confessing Church, because he was never a member of it. [Marahrens was the Bishop of Hanover.]

You put the dismissal of Brother W. from our seminary in this context. During the vacation, Brother W. made contact with Superintendent von Scheven and was already told by him that it would be impossible for him to remain in the seminary if he decided for the General Committee. Brother W.'s decision was preceded by an hour-long discussion before the vacation. He took this step of his own accord and thus withdrew himself.

We are a seminary of the Confessing Church and are subject to the direction of the Councils of Brethren. If anyone loses his confidence in and withdraws his obedience to the leadership, he cannot remain within our seminary. Whether that is equivalent to excommunication I don't know. The Councils of Brethren will have to decide that . . . Brother W. was one of the most intimate and responsible of our brethren. I valued him highly and was very fond of him. We know better than anyone what his departure in that direction means to us. If you had experienced the last two hours which Brother W. spent in the seminary, you would know that it was impossible to say that even one person had accused him of 'faithlessness, cowardice and treachery'. We parted after the most serious pastoral discussion, after a meeting in which I once again said a word to the brethren about the seriousness of the occasion, and after sincere prayer together. It seems to me impermissible to say anything about the inward emotions which seized all of us.

You call all this vindictiveness. I call it 'the truth in love' . . . There is no greater service of love than to put men in the light of the truth of the Word, even when it causes sorrow. There is no vindictiveness here, but only the humble and truly dismayed recognition of the way with which God himself will go with his Word in his Church. The bounds of the Word are also our bounds. We cannot unite where God divides. We can only bear witness to the truth, remain humble and pray for each other.

I now believe that the Holy Spirit spoke at Barmen and Dahlem [the two crucial Synods of the Confessing Church in 1934] which bound themselves to Scripture and Confession alone, a word that is at the same time binding upon us, which thus at the same time draws bounds which we may no longer overlook without being disobedient and from which we can no longer arbitrarily draw back. We can no longer free ourselves from the directing of the Holy Spirit. Now this is also my attitude when I come to a meeting like that at Bredow. I come in certainty and thankfulness that God has let me know the way for his Church through the Word and the Church's Confession. I do not go to such a meeting as to a Quaker meeting, in which each time I should first have to wait for new directions from the Holy Spirit; I go to such a meeting rather as to a battlefield in which the Word of God is in conflict with all human views and would be used as a sharp sword. What takes place here is not a representation of a piece of Christian life, but a struggle for the truth. I do not wait here somehow for an 'intervention of the spirit of God', as you put it. God's spirit battles only through the Word of Scripture and the Church's Confession, and only when my insights are overwhelmed by Scripture and Confession can I know myself to be overwhelmed by the spirit of God. And to this, of course, belongs the open acknowledgement of one's own failings and mistaken ways, and the request for forgiveness. At such moments of responsible decision our attention must remain directed solely towards the truth of the Word of God, and may never be diverted to any human attitude which might be taken up towards it. In just this question of discipline, which lies so near the hearts of both of us, everything seems to me to depend on the left hand not knowing what the right hand is doing, and still more on our noticing all the time, not the disciplined or indisciplined attitude of the other man, but the truth of the testimony. Attention to the truth of the Holy Spirit made known to us is the best guarantee of Christian discipline and makes us free from considering our own attitude, which is in any case inappropriate to this truth. Otherwise we, who would be preachers of love, become through just this the most loveless of judges. The Word of God will judge us. That is enough.

And now to end with, one more serious word. I cannot avoid the impression that your understanding of the Holy Spirit, the Word and the decision of the Church will be used by irresponsible theologians to make room in the Church for any arbitrary, subjective view, so long as it can be described as 'Christian' in its outward form. For you, the Holy Spirit seems to be, not just the reality bound up with the true clear word of Scripture, which inextricably binds us in life and in knowledge, but rather a formative principle of a Christian ideal of life. The Holy Spirit, then, remains somehow neutral. Behind your remarks there lurks a concept of what is 'Christian' which has been won not from the truth of Scripture but from the verdict of human examination. Were that the case, the danger for the Confessing Church would be immeasurably great. The Confessing Church would surrender the promise given to it if any other factor were introduced alongside obedience to the truth, made known by the Holy Spirit in order to give new life to the Church.

[*A letter following disagreement at a conference of clergy held in Stettin-Bredow, 10 January 1936, to clear the air before a critical meeting of the National Confessional Synod, planned for February.*][1]

COSTLY GRACE

Cheap grace is the deadly enemy of our Church. We are fighting today for costly grace. Cheap grace means grace sold on the market like cheapjack's wares. The sacraments, the forgiveness of sin, and the consolations of religion are thrown away at cut prices. Grace is represented as the Church's inexhaustible treasury, from which she showers blessings with generous hands, without asking questions or fixing limits. Grace without price; grace without cost! The essence of grace, we suppose, is that the account has been paid in advance; and, because it has been paid, everything can be had for nothing. Since the cost was infinite, the possibilities of using and spending it are infinite. What would grace be if it were not cheap?

Cheap grace means grace as a doctrine, a principle, a system. It means forgiveness of sins proclaimed as a general truth, the love of God taught as the Christian 'conception' of God. An intellectual assent to that idea is to be held of itself sufficient to secure remission of sins. The church which holds the correct doctrine of grace has, it is supposed, *ipso facto* a part in that grace. In such a church the world finds a cheap covering for its sins; no contrition is required, still less any real desire to be delivered from sin. Cheap grace therefore amounts to a denial of the living Word of God, in fact, a denial of the Incarnation of the Word of God.

Cheap grace means the justification of sin without the justification of the sinner. Grace alone does everything, they say, and so everything can remain as it was before. 'All for sin could not atone.' The world goes on in the same old way, and we are still sinners 'even in the best life' as Luther said. Well, then, let the Christian live like the rest of the world, let him model himself on the world's standards in every sphere of life, and not presumptuously aspire to live a different life under grace from his old life under sin. That was the heresy of the enthusiasts, the Anabaptists and their kind. Let the Christian beware of rebelling against the free and boundless grace of God and desecrating it. Let him not attempt to erect a new religion of the letter by endeavouring to live a life of obedience to the commandments of Jesus Christ! The world has been justified by grace. The Christian knows that and takes it seriously. He knows he must not strive against this indispensable grace. Therefore — let him live like the rest of the world. Of course, he would like to go and do something extraordinary, and it does demand a great deal of restraint to refrain from the attempt, and content himself with living as the world lives!

Yet, it is imperative for the Christian to achieve renunciation, to practise self-effacement, to distinguish his life from the life of the world. He must let grace be grace indeed, otherwise he will destroy the world's faith in the free gift of grace. Let the Christian rest content with his worldliness and with this renunciation of any higher standard than the world. He is doing it for the sake of the world rather than for the sake of grace. Let him be comforted and rest assured in his possession of this grace — for grace alone does everything. Instead of following Christ, let the Christian enjoy the consolations of his grace! That is what we mean by cheap grace, the grace which amounts to the justification of sin without the justification of the repentant sinner, who departs from sin and from whom sin departs. Cheap grace is not the kind of forgiveness of sin which frees us from the toils of sin. Cheap grace is the grace we bestow upon ourselves.

Cheap grace is the preaching of forgiveness without requiring repentance, baptism without church discipline, communion without confession, absolution without personal confession. Cheap grace is grace without discipleship, grace without the cross, grace without Jesus Christ, living and incarnate.

Costly grace is the treasure hidden in the field; for the sake of it a man will gladly go and sell all that he has. It is the pearl of great price to buy which the merchant will sell all his goods. It is the kingly rule of Christ, for whose sake a man will pluck out the eye which causes him to stumble. It is the call of Jesus Christ at which the disciple leaves his nets and follows him.

Costly grace is the Gospel which must be *sought* again and again, the gift that must be *asked* for, the door at which a man must *knock*.

Such grace is *costly* because it calls us to follow, and it is *grace* because it calls us to follow *Jesus Christ*. It is costly because it costs a man his life, and it is grace because it gives a man the only true life. It is costly because it condemns sin, and grace because it justifies the sinner. Above all, it is *costly* because it cost God the life of his Son: 'ye were bought at a price', and what has cost God much cannot be cheap for us. Above all, it is *grace* because God did not reckon his Son too dear a price to pay for our life, but delivered him up for us.

Costly grace is the Incarnation of God. Costly grace is the sanctuary of God; it has to be protected from the world, and not thrown to the dogs. It is therefore the living word, the Word of God which he speaks as it pleases him. Costly grace confronts us as a gracious call to follow Jesus, it comes as a word of forgiveness to the broken spirit and the contrite heart. Grace is costly because it compels a man to submit to the yoke of Christ and follow him; it is grace because Jesus says: 'My yoke is easy and my burden light.'

[*From the opening paragraphs of Part One (Grace and Discipleship) of*

The Cost of Discipleship, *published as* Nachfolge *in 1937, described by Bethge as 'Finkenwalde's own badge of distinction'.*][2]

THE OFFENSIVE ENCOUNTER WITH THE
ECUMENICAL MOVEMENT

The ecumenical movement and the Confessing Church have made an encounter. The ecumenical movement has stood sponsor at the coming-into-being of the Confessing Church, in prayer for her and in commitment to her. That is a fact, even if it is an extremely remarkable fact, which is most offensive to some people. It is extremely remarkable, because an understanding of ecumenical work might *a priori* have been least expected in the circles of the Confessing Church, and an interest in the theological questioning of the Confessing Church might *a priori* have been least expected in ecumenical circles. It is offensive, because it is vexatious to the German nationalist for once to have to see his church from the outside, because no one gladly shows his wounds to a stranger. But it is not only a remarkable and an offensive fact, it is still more a tremendously promising fact, because in this encounter the ecumenical movement and the Confessing Church ask each other the reason for their existence. The ecumenical movement must vindicate itself before the Confessing Church, and the Confessing Church must vindicate itself before the ecumenical movement, and just as the ecumenical movement is led to a serious inward concern and crisis by the Confessing Church, so too the Confessing Church is led to a serious inward concern and crisis by the ecumenical movement. This reciprocal questioning must now be developed.

[*Taken from a paper written in August 1935, in which Bonhoeffer examines the theological basis both of the ecumenical movement and the Confessing Church.*][3]

THE PURPOSES OF THE SEMINARY

The Finkenwalde Seminary is one of five seminaries of the Confessing Church in the Old Prussian Union. It was founded in April 1935. As most of the older seminaries have fallen into the hands of the German Christians, the Confessing Church had itself to see to the regular education of its young theologians. Alongside the old seminaries of Elberfeld and Naumburg am Queiss, which were brought into the Confessing Church by their directors, during the church struggle, seminaries have sprung up in Bielefeld, Finkenwalde and Blöstau in East Prussia.

The task of the seminary is to bring together for six months young theologians who, after the conclusion of their studies and the passing of their first examination, have been doing parish work as curates in the Confessing Church for a year or more. Here they are to think through and work through the basic questions of Holy Scripture, practical work and true evangelical teaching with the co-operation of the director of the seminary. The young brethren will engage in a common Christian life of daily devotions together, quiet times for prayer, and mutual service. In accordance with the situation of the Confessing Church, their life will be one of extreme simplicity, focused on the great office which the brethren are to undertake shortly afterwards with their ordination. But over and above the seminary work proper, a seminary of the Confessing Church is increasingly finding itself being given the important task of taking a practical part in the service of the churches of the region. Only recently our seminary arranged a six-day popular mission in a Pomeranian church district, alongside other regular outside work which is done by a small group of brethren, some ordained who are remaining at the seminary for a longer period and who keep themselves free for any urgent church service.

The theological faculties *of the state* at the moment foster almost without exception either the German Christian heresy or indecision. Thus the rising theological generation is in great danger of no longer coming into contact with a theology decisively based upon the Confession. At the moment, the seminaries of the Confessing Church are almost the only places in which the Confessing Church can in complete independence train people to have an attitude towards doctrine and life that is firmly governed by the Confession. Hitherto the Confessing Church has been bearing the great burden

of the seminaries alone. But it must be our aim that the free forces of the Confessing congregations find themselves more and more ready to understand the seminaries as their own responsibility and contribute towards them, so that the seminaries can continue their work on the basis of free gifts. We are now concerned to build up our seminary entirely on the freewill offerings of a large group of members of congregations. We will be grateful for any help.
[*Explanatory article accompanying an appeal.*][4]

THE SILENT CONTROVERSY WITH KARL BARTH

Since you wrote to me in England that I was to return by the next ship, or failing that by the ship after next, you have heard nothing from me in person. I must ask you to excuse me for that, but the arrow did strike home! I think it really was on the ship after the next that I came home. Now I have been back here eighteen months; in many respects I am glad that I was over there, but I am still glad that I am back here again. There are all sorts of reasons for my not having written since then . . . I wanted first of all to come to some kind of conclusion about the questions which the Bible raised for me and which kept on bothering me, though, of course, I also recognized that I was probably departing from your views. The whole period was basically a constant, silent controversy with you, and so I had to keep silence for a while. The chief questions are those of the exposition of the Sermon on the Mount and the Pauline doctrine of justification and sanctification. I am engaged on a work on the subject (*The Cost of Discipleship*) and would have asked and learnt a very, very great deal from you. Most of us who feel that they had to keep away from you for a while for theological reasons of some sort seem to find that afterwards, in a personal conversation with you, they learn that once again they have seen the whole question in far too crude terms. Now I am earnestly hoping for another opportunity of seeing you and talking to you at length. . . .

Work at the seminary gives me great joy. Academic and practical work are combined splendidly. I find that all along the line the young theologians coming into the seminary raise the very questions that have been troubling me recently, and of course our life together is strongly influenced by this. I am firmly convinced that, in view of what the young theologians bring with them from the university and in view of the independent work which will be demanded of them in the parishes, particularly here in the East, they need a completely different kind of training which life together in a seminary like this unquestionably gives. You can hardly imagine how empty, how completely burnt out most of the brothers are when they come to the seminary. Empty, not only as regards theological insights and still more as regards knowledge of the Bible, but also as regards their personal life. On an open evening — the only one in which I shared —you once said very seriously to the students that you sometimes felt as though you would rather give up all lectures and instead pay a surprise visit to someone and ask him, like old Tholuck, 'How goes it with your soul?' The need has not been met since then, not even by the Confessing Church. But there are very few who recognize this sort of work with young theologians as a task of the Church and do something about it. And it is really what everyone is waiting for. Unfortunately, I am not up to it, but I remind the brothers of each other, and that seems to me to be the most important thing. It is, though, certain that both theological work and real pastoral fellow-ship can only grow in a life which is governed by gathering round the Word morning and evening, and by fixed times of prayer. And it is in fact only the consequence of what you have made very clear in 'Anselm'. The charge of legalism does not seem to me to fit at all. What is there legalistic in a Christian setting to work to learn what prayer is and in his spending a good deal of his time in this learning? A leading man in the Confessing Church once said to me, 'We have no time for meditation now, the ordinands should learn how to preach and to catechize'. That seems to me either a complete misun-derstanding of what young theologians are like today, or culpable ignorance of how preaching and catechism come to life. The ques-tions that are seriously put to us today by young theologians are: How do I learn to pray? How do I learn to read the Bible? If we cannot help them there we cannot help them at all. And there is really nothing obvious about it. To say, 'If someone does not know that, he should not be a minister', would be to exclude most of us from our profession. It is quite clear to me that all these things are justified when alongside them and with them — at just the same time! — there is really serious and sober theological, exegetical and dogmatic work going on. Otherwise all questions are given the wrong emphasis. But I do not mean to ignore these questions; they are what I am concerned with! And they are just the things which I would most have liked to discuss with you.

[*Letter to Karl Barth, 19 September 1936.*][5]

9

THE LAST DAYS OF FINKENWALDE

THE JUDAS SERMON

Matthew 26:45b–50: Jesus had kept one thing from his disciples right up to the Last Supper. He had left them in no doubt about the path of suffering he was to tread. Three times he had told them that the Son of Man had to be delivered into the hands of sinners. But he had not yet revealed the deepest mystery to them. Only in their last hours together in the Passover meal could he say to them, The Son of Man is delivered into the hands of sinners – by treachery. 'One of you will betray me.'

By themselves, the enemy can have no power over him. It takes a friend for that: a close friend to give him up, a disciple to betray him. The most fearful thing of all happens not from outside, but from within. Jesus' path to Golgotha begins with the disciples' betrayal. Some sleep, that incomprehensible sleep in Gethsemane, one betrays him, and in the end 'all the disciples forsook him and fled'.

The night of Gethsemane comes to an end. '*Behold the hour is at hand*' – the hour which Jesus had prophesied earlier, the hour of which the disciples had long known and at whose advent they trembled, the hour for which Jesus was so ready and for which the disciples were so utterly unprepared, the hour which nothing in the world could postpone any longer. 'Behold the hour is at hand, *and the Son of Man is delivered into the hands of sinners.*'

'Delivered', says Jesus. That means that it is not the world that gets him in its grasp. Jesus himself is now handed over, surrendered, given up by his own. He is refused protection. No one will bother with him any more – leave him to the others. That is, Jesus is thrown aside, the protecting hands of his friends are lowered. Let the hands of the sinners do what they will with him now. Let them assault him, those whose impious hands should never have touched him. Let them make sport of him, mock him, smite him. We cannot change that now. This is what delivering up Jesus means, no longer to take his part, to surrender him to mockery and the power of the public, to let the world take its feelings out on him, not to stand by him any more. Jesus is handed over to the world by his own. That is his death.

Jesus knows what is before him. Firmly and decisively he summons his disciples, '*Rise, let us be going*'. Often his threatening foes had to fall back before him, he went out freely through their midst, their hands fell. Then his hour had not yet come. Now it is here. Now he goes out to meet them of his own free will. And so that there shall be no doubt, so that it is absolutely clear that the hour has come in which he is to be delivered up, he says, '*See, my betrayer is at hand*'. Not a glance at the great crowd that is approaching, nor at the swords and clubs of the enemy. By themselves they would have had no power! Jesus fixes his gaze solely on the one who has brought to pass this hour of darkness. His disciples too are to know where the enemy stands. For a moment everything, the history of salvation, the history of the world, lies in the hands of one man – the traitor. 'See, my betrayer is at hand' – and in the darkness the disciples recognize him with horror – Judas, the disciple, the brother, the friend. With horror, for when Jesus that self-same evening had said to them, 'One of you will betray me', none had dared to accuse another. None had been able to imagine another capable of such an action. And so each had to ask the other, 'Lord, is it I?' 'Lord, is it I?' Each in his own heart was more capable than his brother of such an action.

'*While he was still speaking, Judas came, one of the twelve, and with him a great crowd with swords and clubs.*' Now we see only the two persons concerned. The disciples and the mob fall back – both do their work badly. Only two do their work as it had to be done.

Jesus and Judas. Who is Judas? That is the question. It is one of the oldest and most troublesome questions in Christianity. First of all let us keep to what the Evangelist himself tells us about Judas: he is *Judas, one of the twelve*. Can we feel something of the horror with which the Evangelist wrote this tiny clause? Judas, one of the twelve – what more was there to say here? And does this not really say everything? The whole of the dark mystery of Judas, and at the same time the deepest shock at his deed? Judas, one of the twelve. That means that it was impossible for this to happen; it was absolutely impossible – and yet it happened. No, there is nothing more to explain or to understand here. It is completely and utterly inexplicable, incomprehensible, it is an unfathomable riddle – and yet it was done. Judas, one of the twelve. That does not just mean that he was one who was with Jesus day and night, who had followed Jesus, who had sacrificed something, who had given up all to be with Jesus, a brother, a friend, a confidant of Peter, of John, of the Lord himself. It means something far more incomprehensible: Jesus himself called and chose Judas! That is the real mystery. For Jesus knew who would betray him from the beginning. In St John's Gospel Jesus says, 'Did I not choose you, the twelve, and one of you is a devil?' Judas, one of the twelve, and now the reader must look not only at Judas, but rather in great bewilderment at the Lord who chose him. And those whom he chose, he loved. He shared his whole life with them, he shared with them the mystery of his person, and in the same way he sent them out to preach the Gospel. He gave them authority to drive out demons and to heal – and Judas was in their midst. In fact, by his office of keeping charge of the disciples' purse, Judas seemed to have been marked out above the others.

True, John once says that Judas was a thief. But is that not meant to be just a dark hint that Judas was a thief in the case of Jesus, that he stole and surrendered to the world Jesus, who did not belong to him? And are not the thirty pieces of silver, too, simply a sign of how common and small the gift of the world is for him who knows the gift of Jesus? And yet Jesus knew from the beginning who would betray him! John has one more completely mysterious sign of Jesus' closeness with Judas to tell. On the night of the Last Supper, Jesus offers Judas a sop dipped in the dish, and with this sign of the closest community Satan enters into Judas. Thereupon Jesus says to Judas, half as a request, half as a command, 'What you are going to do, do quickly'. No one else understood what was happening. Everything remained between Jesus and Judas.

'*Friend, why are you here?*' Do you hear how Jesus still loves Judas, how he still calls him his friend at this hour? Even now Jesus will not let Judas go. He lets himself be kissed by him. He does not push him away. No, Judas must kiss him. His communion with Jesus must reach its consummation. 'Why are you here?' Jesus knows well why Judas is here, and yet, 'Why are you here?' And 'Judas, would you betray the Son of Man with a kiss?' A last expression of a disciple's faithfulness, coupled with betrayal. A last sign of passionate love, joined with far more passionate hate. A last enjoyment of a subservient gesture, in consciousness of the superiority of the victory over Jesus which it brings. An action divided to its uttermost depths, this kiss of Judas. Not to be able to be abandoned by Christ, and yet to give him up. Judas, would you betray the Son of Man with a kiss? Who is Judas? Should we not also think here of the name that he bore? 'Judas', does he not stand here for the people, divided to its uttermost depths, from which Jesus came, for the chosen people, that had received the promise of the Messiah and yet had rejected him? For the people of Judah, that loved the Messiah and yet could not love him in this way? 'Judas' – his name in German means 'thanks'. Was this kiss not the thanks offered by the divided people and yet at the same time the eternal renunciation? Who is Judas? Who is the traitor? Faced with this question, are we to be able to do anything but say with the disciples, 'Lord, is it I?' 'Is it I?'

'*Then they came and laid hands on Jesus and seized him*'

'Tis I, whose sin now binds thee,
With anguish deep surrounds thee,
And nails thee to the tree;
The torture thou art feeling,
Thy patient love revealing,
'Tis I should bear it, I alone.

Let us now see the final end. At the same hour as Jesus accomplishes his redemptive suffering on the cross on Golgotha, Judas went and hanged himself, damned himself in fruitless repentance. What terrible community! Christendom has always seen in Judas the dark mystery of divine rejection and eternal damnation. It has recognized and borne witness with fear to the earnestness and judgement of God on the traitor. For precisely this reason, however, it has never looked on him with pride and arrogance, but has in trembling and in recognition of its own tremendous sin sung, 'O poor Judas, what is this that thou hast done?' and would take refuge with him who hung upon the cross for all our sins and brought about our redemption, praying,

> In thy most bitter passion,
> My heart to share doth cry,
> With thee for my salvation
> Upon the cross to die.
> Ah, keep my heart thus moved
> To stand thy cross beneath,
> To mourn thee well-beloved
> Yet thank thee for thy death.

[*Sermon preached 14 March 1937.*][1]

WAR AND PEACE

1. The Gospel is the message of peace. 'Christ is our peace.' This peace may be a hidden peace, peace with God, but it must emerge and make an open appearance in the ordering of human society, because Christ's claim to dominion extends over the world.

2. The Church of Christ must affirm this message before the whole world, not only before the Lord's community, but also before the world of nations. The Church may never surrender this worldwide commission, as it is contained in the Gospel, to anyone, 'You are the salt of the earth'.

3. Because of this commission, the Church bears witness to Christendom that in all tensions and all divisions it must allow itself to be guided and supported by faith in the one Lord of the Church and by the commandment, 'If possible, so far as it depends upon you, live peaceably with all'.

4. The Church must recall the nations from worshipping false gods, to obedience towards the only God, the Father of Jesus Christ. The Church must show them that the cross is the sole deliverance from all helplessness, anxiety and sin, and that it is the place from which come new ways of peace.

5. As the Church fulfils this commission today, it must above all remember that even among the 'Christian' nations the national consciousness is being developed into a new national religion and a state cult. On the other hand, not only economic questions, but political, racial and class ideologies of all kinds threaten to tear the world of nations further apart.

6. The Church has shown itself to be fully conscious of its obligations and duties towards the people and the state on the basis of its assessment of them. But it is in love and mercy bound to point out that a new world war would not only bring unprecedented suffering and misery on sorely tried peoples, but also destroy the ethical foundations of international life by its slaughter and by doing away with obedience to all God's commandments.

7. The Church welcomes the serious attempts by statesmen to seek peaceful solutions to conflicting national interests and also to find ways of providing international aid in basic necessities, all of which serve to keep the peace.

8. The Church, then, appeals to Christendom and to the nations, for peace. But for the sake of true peace and to make clear the issues involved, the Church must also point out that an external peace

alone cannot represent the fulfilment of God's will. Even in struggling for peace, we can be threatened by the temptation of arbitrary and godless thought and action, and by the demonic character of our time. The Church knows that the fulfilment of the message 'peace on earth' will always be the subject of Christian hope until the appearing of Jesus Christ.

9. A war is always a severe trial for the Church. At the same time it is a call for the Church to prove its faith and obedience towards its Lord. For this very reason, even if war comes, the ecumenical alliance of the Church of Christ must not collapse. It must bear its witness in the fellowship of faith, love and intercession. The bonds of the Holy Spirit are stronger than the bonds of the created world. [*Written in April 1937 in preparation for the ecumenical conference on 'Church, Community and State', to be held in Oxford, July 1937. These points are his summary at the end of the preparatory paper.*][2]

THE OLYMPIC GAMES, BERLIN, AUGUST 1936

Bonhoeffer, 31 July: I am lecturing for the Olympiade on Wednesday, at 5 in the afternoon, 'The Inner Life of the German Evangelical Church since the Reformation'. In half an hour! I am making a collection of hymns: Luther, Gerhardt, Zinzendorf, Gellert. It isn't easy . . . . Jacobi, Asmussen, Dibelius and Niemöller are speaking as well as myself. They reacted so strongly against my attempt to drop out that I must go on with it now. I must do some church history for my lecture. Yesterday it was Zinzendorf and I was very depressed at the end of it! What rottenness there is beneath all this piety. I tell you that I found things there that I am almost embarrassed to repeat to you. And all this in hymns too! Yes, that's man! pious man! . . . We need the fresh air of the Word to keep us clean and still we cannot leap outside of ourselves. But enough of this, away with human eyes! It is disgusting!

REPORT OF THE LECTURE IN CHRISTLICHE WELT
BY HANS SCHLEMMER

While the lectures given in the church of the Holy Trinity were
academically satisfying, they were hardly well attended; those in St
Paul's [where Bonhoeffer was lecturing] were the opposite of this.
Night after night, the enormous church was not only filled to overflowing, but parallel meetings had also to be held in another large
church to cope with the visitors. Dr Bonhoeffer struck the same
tone as Dr Jacobi had done and illustrated his exposition with a
number of hymns. According to him, the decline began as early as
Paul Gerhardt: Pietism, the Enlightenment and the Nineteenth
Century sink lower and lower. Only in the present and especially in
the hymns of Heinrich Vogel (!) do we begin to rise again to the
heights of the Reformation. The speaker tried to prove his thesis by
means of selected hymns and was even successful because of the
complete arbitrariness of his selection. He did not shrink from
quoting the first half of a verse when the second half, left unquoted,
made the opposite point. When we consider that here we have a
pupil of Harnack, we can only deplore this treatment of history. The
third speaker, Professor Iwand of Königsberg, followed much the
same line. To sum up: in Holy Trinity, valuable theology developed
in a scholarly way, but a very small audience; in St Paul's, narrow and
very suspect theology, but great religious enthusiasm and vast
congregations, listening with the deepest devotion. This state of
affairs must cause great alarm among those concerned with the
future of the Evangelical Church.

BONHOEFFER'S OWN REPORT TO EBERHARD BETHGE,

6 *August:* Yesterday evening was very good. The church filled to
overflowing, people sitting on the altar steps and standing all
around. I wish I could have preached instead of giving a lecture!
Some 1500 or 2000 people and an overflow service. I was taken from
one church to another by car in grand style! In one bookshop, I saw a
placard:

After the Olympiade,
We'll stew the Confessing Church to marmalade!
The day the Jews are kicked out,
The Confessing Church won't cock a snout!

Lovely poetry! An American took a photograph of it and has sent it home. So he told Niemöller. . . .

If we could have met, there would have been so much else of importance to discuss which I cannot entrust to a letter – extremely important church matters. At the moment, I can only say this, we should try to remain in Switzerland beyond the time of the conference (the Universal Council for Life and Work, meeting in Chamby to prepare for the Oxford Conference on Church, Community and State). This can be very important. I have applied for money, which must do for both of us. We may have to remain there for an extra ten days. Be prepared for that and stay somewhere near the conference. Please do not speak to anyone about this![3]

BONHOEFFER'S REPORT OF FINKENWALDE'S
ONLY COMPLETE YEAR, 1936

'He has done all things well.' That is what we should say at the end of this year about every week, every hour that is past. We should go to pray with this word until there is no longer an hour of which we did not want to say 'He has done all things well'. Those very days which were hard to us, which troubled us and worried us, days which have left behind in us a trace of bitterness, should not fade from our minds today until we have been able to confess humbly and thankfully even of them. 'He has done all things well.' We should not forget, but overcome. That happens through giving thanks. We should not solve the insoluble riddle of the past and sink into fretful grumbling, but leave even the incomprehensible as it is and surrender it peacefully into God's hands. That is done through humility. 'He has done all things well.'

But the most fearful torment still remains: My guilt! my guilt! My negligence in my office, my unfaithfulness in serving the community, my ungratefulness, my anger, my idleness at prayer, my utterly stubborn, despairing and unhappy heart – what about that? The evil fruits of my sin have influence without end. How am I to put an end to it? And yet you are no Christian, but only harden yourself in your sin, if you cannot say even of your guilt, 'He has done all things well'. That does not mean that *we* have done all things well. Do you believe it? It is the ultimate, the most astonishing recognition of the Christian that in the end he can say even of his sin, He has done all things well. He has helped me to find him even through my sin. He has finally covered all my sin.

Only now do we rightly know the meaning of 'He has done all things well'. He has healed us. He was there and at work all the time. Only now, too, can we truly thank him for the glory of our office, for our work, for the daily Word, for brotherly fellowship, for all kind of personal help and guidance, for the preservation of body and soul from all manner of great evil and danger. Now all the past is swallowed up in one joy, He has done all things well.

Over the past year, God the Lord has deigned to give our Confessing Church great questions, great tasks and great sufferings. Since the intervention of the state church committees in the life of our church, the Confessing Church has suffered great shocks. There have been hard decisions for you, dear brethren, in the parishes. You have had to lead the struggle and in so doing have gone through much questioning, doubt and temptation. Our service here in the house was able to consist chiefly in continuing our work quietly and straightforwardly. Our way was shown clearly.

We have been assembling together every day in the old way to pray, to read the Bible and to praise our God, and as we have done so we have thought of you. Similarly at the end of the day there have been devotions and intercessions for all the concerns of our Church, for your work and your struggle. You know that we have joined with you all in our daily time of meditation and have prayed for one another before God. It was a great delight to us that over and above the confines of our brotherhood some members of congregations far and near have also joined our meditations, and we should also keep them in our thoughts. We should also let ourselves be reminded to keep up faithfully the morning half-hour each day, for considering the Scriptures and interceding. Each of us knows the needs, the inner contradiction, the laziness, which keep on wanting to hold us up, and how to search out what we have recognized as our salvation. We have still been given time and admonition. If one person goes astray, that is a visible or invisible weakening of every one else in the fellowship of prayer. Let us not despise God's gift. As well as meditation, however, daily and plentiful reading of Scripture must keep its place. No day of our life in office may go past without reading the Bible. The very controversies of the last months have once again clearly shown to our shame how unversed in Scripture we still are. How ready people were to make the decision for or against the church committees dependent on all sorts of contingencies of this or that kind, instead of asking for and seeking out the evidence of Scripture. Indeed, how little did people listen when the Bible was read out, and how readily they swallowed all our novelties. This must be changed. We must make it a rule to look for the scriptural evidence for every decision that confronts us, and not to rest until we have found it. Our confidence in dealing with the Bible must increase year by year. And there is something else. We know that it was quite a long time before some of the brothers who were arrested were given Bibles. Weeks like that can prove whether we have been faithful in our reading of Scripture and whether in our knowledge of Scripture we have acquired a great treasury.

Lectures and exercises stand now, as ever, under the shadow of biblical work. After dealing with 'The Discipleship of Christ' in the first course, the theme 'The Visible Church' followed in the second, 'The New Life, in Paul' in the third, and 'Concrete Ethics, in Paul' in the present semester. It would take too long to tell you about the Old Testament, homilectic and catchetical work. A great deal of theological work has been done, from the first course onwards, but I believe a certain climax has been reached in it with the present course. While I am writing this report, a two-and-a-half-day-long disputation is going on, from morning to evening, on 'The preaching of the Law'. For some weeks a chosen group of brothers has been working all their free time to prepare this disputation. We can be grateful for the clarification and the furthering of our knowledge and our insights in many important spheres. But at the same time, our community is knit more closely together by this common work on a question which is so significant for our Church today.

We have made music, as ever, with great joy. In default of any instruments in Zingst [the first, provisional location of the seminary], the first course was predominantly active in singing. The second course at Finkenwalde had two grand pianos and tremendous soloists! On the third Sunday in Advent we had a musical evening for the parish and the friends of the house, which was repeated in the church at Podejuch. We were able to assemble quite a respectable orchestra for it. It was a great delight to all of us, and I for one cannot imagine our common life here without daily music-making together. We have certainly driven out some evil spirits that way.

Although the quietness of domestic life and work must be the real purpose of the short time at the seminary, each course has also had a glimpse of life beyond our walls. In the spring, we accepted an invitation to Sweden. For most people this trip was the first encounter with the Church of Christ beyond the borders of Germany, with the ecumenical world. We were given a most hearty welcome, and ten days were almost overfilled with seeing, hearing and meetings. The friendship and the love we found there enriched us on our return. We are all grateful for this visit. In the same way, the summer course went, for about the same period, to a popular mission together in the Belgard district. Four brethren each were housed in six villages; they preached on four evenings of the week and on Sunday. In the evening these four each expounded a text for ten minutes. This combined proclamation, which derives from shared daily work in the parish and shared prayer, commended itself to all the brethren involved and, we hope, to the parish. After long weeks of silence it is a special delight to preach the Gospel again. So this popular mission week has strongly influenced the semester. One special benefit from this week has been that since then we have kept close contact with several parishes and a number of people, and that we are continually given indications of Christian love and readiness to help. We have much reason for gratitude.

Several mission weeks have been requested for this winter semester; the brethren of the community have always held some and will hold more. We hope to have another popular mission to one of the districts here with the whole seminary at the end of January.

It was a special delight to have the older brethren with us again for their annual reunion at the beginning of the last two semesters. Despite some abnormality and unrest which this produces at the beginning of the semester, it is good for the older and the younger brethren to get to know each other in this way, and it makes settling in much easier for the new course. We had busy and happy days of reunion. Time at the seminary is so short, and the gap between life in the seminary and the solitariness of work in a village is so great and brings with it such important questions, that this yearly meeting is an urgent necessity and a real help. Of course, there are individual letters and visits in between. Reports of brethren on their work have already grown into quite a large volume, and are studied thoroughly by brethren who visit us from time to time. We also try to serve the brethren in parishes by the circular letter which goes out from the house each month, by the short report on the house, the goings-on of the older brothers, the notification of texts for meditation and preaching aids. But all this only gains its full value through the annual reunions. Let us keep to them.

During the year almost all the brethren from the first and second courses have been ordained. We have been thinking of you particularly on these days. God grant you a great love for your parish and the strength to preach the uncurtailed Gospel.

We do not want to end this survey without thinking of the three brethren who during the course of this year have cut themselves off from our church and have put themselves at the disposal of the church committees. This has been a great grief to us. Our words here have no longer been enough. And in their life and their office we commend them to God in prayer.

The group of parishes and friends which gives regular help to our house has grown. We recognize here the gracious guidance of God, who by this leads us even more to recognize our own failings and to give thanks. Many gifts have shamed us. We have been done great services. They summon us to be even more faithful to our work than before.

There is the report. Much has happened and yet we recognize that we have done nothing worth mentioning before God. We acknowledge that everywhere we have lagged far behind what should have been done. We owe much to our office and to each other. So once again we will let ourselves be surrounded by his forgiving love and thankfully confess: Not we, but HE has done all things well. And as we look to the New Year we hear, 'Commend your ways unto the Lord and hope on him, HE will do all things well'.

[*Circular letter sent to all students from Finkenwalde, 21 December 1936.*]

1937   1 July, arrest of Martin Niemöller
         September, Finkenwalde closed by order of Himmler
         November – 27 men from Finkenwalde arrested
1938   February – Bonhoeffer's first contact with the leaders of the
         political resistance to Hitler
         20 June – Finkenwalde reunion at Zingst

ADVENT LETTER 1938

At the end of the old church year and the beginning of the new, my first greeting to you is the saying from last week's meditation text: 'May the God of steadfastness and encouragement grant you to live in such harmony with one another, in accord with Christ Jesus' (Romans 15:5). We have been doing a great deal of work here recently, thinking together about the New Testament concept of patience, during which it has become quite clear to me that all along the line we have got to the point where there is only one fundamental question. Do we want to learn the meaning of patience from the Gospel? In my opinion, we do not need to take so seriously the numerous questions about which we get impatient. The only serious thing is that our impatience always wants to play nasty tricks on us, by giving itself out as a special kind of obedience, and leading us into unfaithfulness. Somehow, I'm not quite sure how, we have got into a way of thinking which is positively dangerous. We think that we are acting particularly responsibly if every other week we take another look at the question whether the way in which we have set out is the right one. It is particularly noticeable that such a 'responsible reappraisal' always begins the moment serious difficulties appear. We then speak as though we no longer had a 'proper joy and certainty' about this way, or, still worse, as though God and his Word were no longer as clearly present with us as they used to be. In all this, we are ultimately trying to get round what the New Testament calls 'patience' and 'testing'. Paul, at any rate, did not begin to reflect whether his way was the right one when opposition and suffering threatened, nor did Luther. They were both quite certain and glad that they should remain disciples and followers of their Lord. Dear brethren, our real trouble is not doubt about the way upon which we have set out, but our failure to be patient, to keep quiet. We still cannot imagine that today God really doesn't want anything new from us, but simply to prove us in the old way. That is too petty, too monotonous, too undemanding for us. And we simply cannot be constant with the fact that God's cause is not always the successful one, that we really could be 'unsuccessful' and yet be on the right road. This is where we find out whether we have begun in faith or in a burst of enthusiasm.

The significance of patience in the New Testament is quite striking. Only the patient man receives the promise (Matthew 24:13), only the patient man brings forth good fruit (Luke 8:15). A faith which does not become patient is inauthentic, unusable. Faith must be proved. It can only be proved in suffering. Only suffering and endurance will produce the 'perfect' work (James 1:3ff). If we remember that the word faith (*pistis*) already contains the element of faithfulness, we shall not be surprised at the close connection between faith and patience. There is patience only 'in

Jesus' (Revelation 1:9), for Jesus was patient as he bore the cross. Hebrews 12:2 describes Jesus' way of the cross as a way of endurance, of patience. For us endurance means to stand in the fellowship of Christ's suffering (1 Corinthians 1:6ff) and thereby to gain assurance. If we share in the patience of Jesus, we shall ourselves become patient and we will finally have a share in his kingdom (2 Timothy 2:12). The way to patience leads through discipline (2 Peter 1:6). The freer we are from ease and indolence and personal claims, the more ready we shall be for patience.

Our text tells us that we can remain united only if we remain patient. Impatience makes for division. And unfortunately it cannot be denied that all those who have already gone their own way through impatience, have made the struggle and test of patience still more difficult for the other brethren. Impatience disrupts fellowship. In the view of the Gospel, it is not just a minor, venial, bad habit; it is a failure in the testing of faith. Now the God of patience – the God who himself endured in Jesus Christ and helps us to endure – give you 'one mind' – to stand by one another in these hours of testing, to come closer to one another, to strengthen and help one another. It is grim if anyone departs at such a time. But our patience depends, not upon men, but upon Jesus Christ and his patience on the cross. He bore the impatience of all men and so can forgive them. 'One mind', i.e. not this way today and another tomorrow: remain firm by what you already know, remain constant, show yourselves faithful. How little importance we attach to constancy, firmness and faithfulness! In the Scriptures they are right at the top of the list.

God grant them to us by making us patient and promising us his comfort in our endurance. One in patience, one in comfort. We belong together in endurance, we also belong together in comfort and in the final victory. No one fights the battle of proving his faith alone. In the hour in which our patience is tried we are one with those who are of one mind with us. And above all, we know that we are one in the patience and comfort of Jesus. He is our patience and our comfort. And this will also be so in the new church year.

If I may give you some advice, take care and work hard with us at

the concepts with which we are concerned at the moment, temptation, patience, proving, humility, thanksgiving, joy, peace, discipline.
We have to learn to hear the Gospel all over again in these passages.
We are being led through the Scriptures along almost untrodden
paths, but the views are indescribably wide and beautiful. The meditation texts in the next few weeks should also help us here.

During the past few days I have been reading and thinking a great
deal about Psalm 74, Zechariah 2:12, Romans 9:4f and 11:11–15.
That takes us right into prayer.

I have been very glad to hear from many of you and also to have
been able to read your sermons. May I ask the brethren to whom I
return sermons to let me know, at least by a postcard, whether they
arrive safely, and whether you agree with my comments or not?
Please do not think that I cannot be reached by letter, but keep
writing and tell me what happens. I think that I have become better
at answering in the last few months, and at any rate I have taken care
in this direction, for one should not let such comradeship dissolve
through idleness. Above all, keep up the links between yourselves,
write and visit. That is the most important thing. I wish you a good
Advent with all my heart. God bless your preaching and all your
work. May he protect you and your homes. We think of you daily.
[*One of the letters by which Bonhoeffer kept his scattered students, past
and present, in fellowship with him and with each other – Finkenwalde
by correspondence.*][5]

10

THE SAFETY AND SECURITY
OF AMERICA

May I just let you know that I have arrived in London last night.
Would you be so kind as to let me know any time when I could see
you once more before returning to Germany?

In order not to take too much of your time when we meet, I should
like to put before you the two questions which I am very anxious to
discuss with you before my return to Germany. The first question
concerns the Confessing Church, the second one is very personal.
Please excuse my troubling you again and again and my placing one
burden after another on your shoulders.

With regard to the position of the Confessing Church we feel
strongly in Germany that – mainly owing to travelling difficulties –
the relationship of our church to the churches abroad is not as it
ought to be. The responsibility which is placed upon us makes it
more and more necessary to have a permanent exchange of opinion
and the advice of other churches. We are fully aware of and gratefully
appreciate what is continuously being done for us from individuals
to individuals. But I think we must try to go a step farther and come
to some sort of regular co-operation with and to a better representation of the Confessing Church in the ecumenical movements. If we
are not going to take a decisive step forward in this direction I am
afraid that we shall very soon be cut off entirely from our brethren
abroad, and that would at any rate mean a tremendous loss to us.
What I therefore think we should try to get, is a man who could
devote all his time to establishing the necessary contacts, to co-
operating in the ecumenical meetings and conferences, learning and

contributing. I think we failed in earlier years to give our full assistance in advice and fellowship to the Russian Christians; now a similar situation is clearly developing in Germany. Do you not think, my Lord Bishop, it is urgently necessary to avoid a similar failure? Frankly and with all due respects, the German representatives in Geneva simply cannot represent the cause of the Confessing Church. So there is a real vacancy which must be filled sooner or later. This is the first question which I should like to raise and discuss with you before I go home again to see the men of the Brethren Council. I have also an idea in my mind for the eventual financial difficulties.

The second point is of entirely personal character and I am not certain if I may bother you with it. Please, do take it quite apart from the first point. I am thinking of leaving Germany some time. The main reason is the compulsory military service to which the men of my age (1906) will be called up this year. It seems to me conscientiously impossible to join in a war under the present circumstances. On the other hand, the Confessing Church as such has not taken any definite attitude in this respect and probably cannot take it as things are. So I should cause a tremendous damage to my brethren if I would make a stand on this point which would be regarded by the regime as typical of the hostility of our church towards the state. Perhaps the worst thing of all is the military oath which I should have to swear. So I am rather puzzled in this situation, and perhaps even more because I feel that it is really only on Christian grounds that I find it difficult to do military service under the present conditions, and yet there are only very few friends who would approve of my attitude. In spite of much reading and thinking concerning this matter I have not yet made up my mind what I would do under different circumstances. But actually as things are I should have to do violence to my Christian conviction, if I would take up arms 'here and now'. I have been thinking of going to the Mission Field, not as an escape out of the situation, but because I want to serve somewhere where service is really wanted. But here also the German foreign exchange situation makes it impossible to send workers abroad.

With respect to British Missionary Societies, I have no idea of the possibilities there. On the other hand I still have the greatest desire to serve the Confessing Church as long as I possibly could. My Lord Bishop, I am very sorry to add trouble to your trouble, but I thought I might speak freely to you and might ask your advice. You know the Confessing Church and you know me a bit. So I thought you could help me best. It was with regard to this matter that I wanted to see Visser 't Hooft too.

[*After the visit to Chichester, Bonhoeffer wrote again – 13 April 1939.*]

Before I return to Germany I just want to thank you once again for the great help you gave me in our talk at Chichester. I do not know what will be the outcome of it all, but it means much to me to realize that you see the great conscientious difficulties with which we are faced.

[*These letters led to an invitation to lecture in America.*][1]

THE JOURNEY TO AMERICA
(LETTERS TO EBERHARD BETHGE)

7 June: Many thanks for your last letter which pleased me very much just as it was. I will write a letter to you either during the course of the day or tomorrow. This card is to send you all my last best wishes before we get on the Atlantic and there is no more post. We have just left Southampton and will be docking at Cherbourg in a couple of hours. My cabin is very roomy, and everywhere else there is a remarkable amount of space on the ship. The weather is glorious and the sea quite calm, so we were able to lunch without danger. Now there are five quiet days in front of us in which I shall be thinking of you and all the brethren. I still keep wondering how it has all happened. I'm already very much looking forward to your visit to me. I have seen Uncle George and Julius and have made all the arrangements for the autumn. I hope it comes off. Sabine [Dietrich's twin sister] sends her best wishes and thinks back with great pleasure to our visit together. Every joy and blessing in your work.

8 June: Zechariah 7:9: 'Render true judgement, show kindness and mercy each to his brother.' Matthew 5:7: 'Blessed are the merciful for they shall obtain mercy.' Yesterday evening, shortly after I had written, I met a young American theologian, an old Union man [i.e. Union Theological Seminary, New York]. It was like the answer to a prayer. We spoke of Christ in Germany and America, and in Sweden from where he had just come. The task in America!

'Render true judgement and . . . .' That is what I would ask of you first, my brethren at home. I do not want to be given special consideration in your thoughts. But before the merciful God, before the cross of Jesus Christ, what is to render true judgement if not to be merciful? No blind mercy, for that would not be merciful, but a seeing, forgiving, brotherly mercy as the true judgement on us.

'Render true judgement and . . . .' That is a necessary warning and an indication of the task in America. It forbids any pride and makes the task a great one. We must see in the others brethren who are equally under the mercy of Jesus Christ and no longer live and speak for our own particular knowledge or experience; then we will not be prelatical, but merciful. May God remain merciful to us!

9 June: Isaiah 41:9: 'You are my servant, I have chosen you and not cast you off.' John 12:26: 'If any one serves me, he must follow me; and where I am there shall my servant be also.' God chooses the sinner to be his servant so that his grace shall be quite plain. The sinner is to do his work and to extend his grace. God gives work to the one whom he has forgiven. But this work can only consist in discipleship. Great programmes always lead us only to the place at which we ourselves are; but we should be where he is. Indeed, we cannot be anywhere but where he is. You may be working over there and I may be working in America, but we are both only where he is. He brings us together. Or have I missed the place where he is for me? No, God says, 'You are my servant'.

10 June: Psalm 28:7: 'The Lord is my strength and my shield; in him my heart trusts; so I am helped and my heart exults, and with my song

I give thanks to him.' Ephesians 4:30: 'And do not grieve the Holy Spirit of God, in whom you were sealed for the day of redemption.'

In what can 'the heart exult' but in the daily certainty that God is our loving Father and Jesus Christ is our Saviour? What can be more grief to the Holy Spirit than that we indulge in gloomy thoughts and do not entrust ourselves quite confidently to his guidance, his language and his comfort? Until the day of redemption is there, is finally there.

11 June: Psalm 44:21: 'He knows the secrets of the heart.' 1 Corinthians 13:12: 'Now, I know in part; then I shall understand fully, even as I have been fully understood.'

Today is Sunday. No service. The hours have already shifted so much that I cannot share in your service at the same time. But I am altogether with you, today more than ever. If only the doubts about my own course had been overcome. One's own searching into the depths of one's heart, which is nevertheless unfathomable. 'He knows the secrets of the heart.' When the confusion of accusations and excuses, of desires and fears, makes everything within us so obscure, he sees quite clearly into all our secrets. And at the heart of them all he finds a name which he himself has inscribed: Jesus Christ. So, too, one day we shall see quite clearly into depths of the divine heart, and there we shall then be able to read, no, see, a name: Jesus Christ. So we would celebrate Sunday. One day we shall know and see what today we believe; one day we shall hold a service together in eternity.

> The beginning and the end, O Lord, are thine;
> The span between, life, was mine.
> I wandered in the darkness and did not discover myself;
> With thee, O Lord, is clarity, and light is thy house.
> A short time only, and all is done;
> Then the whole struggle dies away to nothing.
> Then I will refresh myself by the waters of life,
> And will talk with Jesus for ever and ever.

This afternoon I had a conversation with a former member of the Harnack Seminar, Fräulein Dr Ferber. She is in charge of an information bureau on the *Bremen*. We had a good talk.

12 June: Deuteronomy 6:6: 'And these words which I command you this day shall be upon your heart. . . .' Acts 15:40: 'Paul departed, being commended by the brethren to the grace of the Lord.'

'Paul departed, being commended by the brethren to the grace of the Lord.' Arrival in New York. To know that brethren have commended us to the grace of the Lord was, in these first few hours, decisive. Rev. Macy from the Federal Council of Churches met me at the pier. First night in Parkside Hotel. Dr Sch. called for me in the evening. I began to see all the problems of German emigration. . . .
[*The Scripture texts are taken from* Losungen, *a daily guide to Bible reading and prayer, compiled by the Moravians and widely used in Germany.*][2]

MISUNDERSTANDING AND RETURN

15 June: Bonhoeffer to Leiper
I wish to thank you very much indeed for the reception you gave me on my arrival in New York. I felt quite at home when Mr Macy gave me your kind letter and when I met you the next morning. It is a great thing to have good friends and fellow Christians abroad.

These beautiful days at Dr Coffin's country home are giving me some time to think about my future, and I am sure you will understand that I should like to put the situation before you as I see it, and ask your advice. Before I left Germany I had long talks with my brethren from the Brethren Council and pledged myself to return to Germany after about a year's time to take up the training work in the Confessing Church again, unless some unforeseen development would change the whole situation. At first they were very reluctant to let me go at all, since they are in need of teachers. It was only when I expressed my hopes that I could be of some use to them by establishing contact with American theologians and churchmen through lectures or meetings, that they gave me leave. So from the point of view of the Confessing Church my trip to America was meant to be an ecumenical link between our isolated church in Germany and our friends over here. We all felt that to be very essential from many points of view. My personal question and difficulty with regard to military service, etc., came in only as a secondary consideration. Of course, my colleagues were glad, that I would be able to postpone my decision for at least one year. Now, I am sure, all that could not be made quite clear in correspondence before I left Germany. But before we are going to work out my programme for the immediate future, however long that will be, I feel strongly that everything ought to be quite clear between us. I deeply appreciate, and so did my friends, the readiness with which you invited me to come to this country and I am most happy indeed to be here again and to meet old friends. There are, however, a few questions which we have to clear up before I start my work over here, and I wish you would help me to do the right thing. The post which you are kindly intending to confer upon me attracts me from every point of view. I feel strongly the necessity of that spiritual help for our refugees. When I was pastor in London I spent most of my time with these people and I felt it was a great privilege to do so. At the same time that post would offer me an unusual opportunity for getting acquainted with the life of the Church in this country, which has been one of my greatest hopes for my stay over here. The only thing that makes me hesitate at the present moment of decision is the question of loyalty to my people at home. All of us, of course, were well aware of the fact that it means running a risk for a Confessing pastor to go to America with the intention of going back to Germany, and we all agreed that I should take that risk and pay the price for it, if necessary, if it is of a true value to the Church of Christ there and here. But, of course, I must not, for the sake of loyalty to the Confessing Church, accept a post which in principle would make my return to Germany impossible. Now, my question is whether that would not be the case with any post that is officially concerned with refugee work? As a matter of fact, I am afraid it would be so. Now, if that is true, what can we do about it? Is there a possibility of giving that post a somewhat larger scope? I have no particular idea, but if, for instance, it were possible to interpret that post as a sort of invitation, as a 'guest post', from the Federation of Churches, to enable me to get acquainted with the church activities in New York and to co-operate in some respect (whereby, of course, some of that pastoral work of which you have been thinking might be conferred upon me on the respective occasions), I think that would change the matter a good deal. But, of course, I have no idea under what heading such a thing could be done. This is the first point, which I should very much like to have your advice on.

Secondly, when Reinhold Niebuhr wrote me first in February he was hoping to provide a few lectureships for me all over the country, so as to give me an opportunity of seeing a good deal of the theological schools and of getting in contact with the professors of theology. That, of course, would be very much in the line of my work in Germany and I would be greatly interested to do that sort of work. Now, do you suppose that the post in New York would leave the necessary time to do some investigation and some visiting of that sort?

Finally, let me add a very personal remark. My best friend in Germany, a young Confessing pastor, who has been working with me for many years, will be in the same conflict with regard to military service, etc., at the latest by next spring, possibly in the fall of this year. I feel it would be an utmost disloyalty to leave him alone in Germany when the conflict comes up for him. I should either have to go back to stand by him and to act with him, or to get him out and share my living with him. Whatever it be, though, I do not know if he would be willing to leave Germany. That is a last personal, but not only personal reason, why I feel bound to keep my way back open. I am sure you will appreciate that this is a duty of *Bruderschaft* which in these times one simply has to fulfil.

Now I have put my case before you. I know I am causing you a great deal of trouble with all that. But you know us Germans and that we are sometimes a little complicated, and more than that, you know the Confessing Church and its needs. . . . If you should think it impossible to find the right post for me, please feel entirely free to tell me and then we should try to make the best of the next few months and I should return to Germany, certainly very grateful for all the friendship I have experienced over here again in the latter part of the fall. My friends at home would only be too glad if I came back a little earlier than expected. But if you would see a way through all these difficulties, then I shall stay here with great pleasure, interest and gratefulness.

19 June: I have just received a letter from Dr Freudenberg asking me urgently not to take over the refugee post if I wish to go back to Germany. He also calls my attention to the fact that there are many of our Confessing pastors who will never be able to return to Germany and from whom, therefore, I should not take away the chance of this post. I hope you will be able to spare an hour of your time tomorrow for me.

BONHOEFFER TO NIEBUHR: JULY 1939

. . . Sitting here in Dr Coffin's garden I have had the time to think and to pray about my situation and that of my nation and to have God's will for me clarified. I have come to the conclusion that I have made a mistake in coming to America. I must live through this difficult period of our national history with the Christian people of Germany. I will have no right to participate in the reconstruction of Christian life in Germany after the war if I do not share the trials of this time with my people. My brethren in the Confessing Synod wanted me to go. They may have been right in urging me to do so; but I was wrong in going. Such a decision each man must make for himself. Christians in Germany will face the terrible alternative of either willing the defeat of their nation in order that Christian civilization may survive, or willing the victory of their nation and thereby destroying our civilization. I know which of these alternatives I must choose; but I cannot make that choice in security . . .

DIARY FRAGMENT

7 July: Last day in New York. Paul tried to keep me back. It's no good. Van Dusen lecture. Pack. With Hans Wedell before lunch. Theological conversation with Paul. Farewell in the seminary. Supper with Van Dusen. Go to the ship with Paul. Farewell half-past eleven, sail at half-past twelve. Manhattan by night; the moon over the skyscrapers. It is very hot. The visit is at an end. I am glad to have been over and glad that I am on the way home. Perhaps I have learnt more in this month than in a whole year nine years ago; at least I have acquired some important insight for all future decisions. Probably this visit will have a great effect upon me.

9 July: Since I have been on the ship my inner uncertainty about the future has ceased. I can think of my shortened visit to America without reproaches. Reading: 'It is good for me that I was afflicted, that I might learn thy statutes' (Psalm 119:71). One of my favourite verses from my favourite psalm.

BONHOEFFER TO CHICHESTER (LONDON, 22 JULY)

. . . It was a difficult decision, but I am still convinced, I was not allowed to decide otherwise. That meant my early return to Germany. Kindly enough, I was invited by Dr Coffin and Van Dusen to stay at Union Seminary as long as I wanted. But when news from Danzig reached me I felt compelled to go back as soon as possible and to make my decisions in Germany. I do not regret my trip to USA . . . though, of course, it had been taken under different presuppositions. I have seen and learnt much in the few weeks over there and I am looking forward to my work in Germany again. What sort of personal decisions will be asked from me I do not know. But nobody knows that now.

My passport expires next spring; it is therefore uncertain when I shall be in this country again. Let me thank you today for all help and friendship and real understanding in the past and in the future. We shall never forget you during the coming events. I thank you for what you have done for my brother-in-law and his family [Bonhoeffer's twin sister, Sabine, married to Gerhard Leibholz, and their two children]. It has meant everything to them. Will you allow me to leave them in this country with the confidence that they may approach you whenever they need advice and help? Of course, their future is uncertain too, and it will require much patience and much energy before they can start afresh. Nevertheless, I am confident that they will not suffer more than they can bear.

[*Sections from many letters and diary entries during this critical period.*][3]

11

Pastoral Care in Wartime

20 September, 1939: In answer to an official question, I have received the news that our dear brother Theodor Maass was killed in Poland on 3 September (1939). You will be as stunned by this news as I was. But, I beg you, let us thank God in remembrance of him. He was a good brother, a quiet, faithful pastor of the Confessing Church, a man who lived from word and sacrament, whom God has also thought worthy to suffer for the Gospel. I am sure that he was prepared to go. Where God tears great gaps we should not try to fill them with human words. They should remain open. Our only comfort is the God of the resurrection, the Father of our Lord Jesus Christ, who was and is his God. In him we know our brothers and in him is the abiding fellowship of those who have overcome and those who still await their hour. God be praised for our dead brother and be merciful to us all at our end. The parents of brother Maass live at Stralsund, Pastor Maass, Ketelhotstrasse, 8.

I know that the following brothers are now with the army: [Here follows a list of 16 and further list of 9, whom he expects are in the army, but he has no army post office number for them]. Others are likely to be called up at any moment. Please let me know as soon as anyone is called up, or if there is someone not on the list whom I ought to know about. Let me know all the army post office numbers that you have. And take time to write to the brethren out there as often as possible. And above all, we must not neglect the greatest service that is left to us, our faithful daily intercession. There is so much that we must ask for our brethren with the army, but first and last always this, that at all times they may show themselves to be Christians, that they may do a real service to many of their comrades, and that Jesus Christ may be their sole comfort both in life and in death.

Many of us have been inwardly disquieted during the past few weeks. We know that our brethren are out there in all sorts of battles and dangers, we hear of the death of a brother, and we feel an urge, 'I too must be where my brethren are, I don't want anything more than they have'. This often weighs us down completely, and then everything that we do seems so superfluous. Indeed, even the questions about the life of our Church, for which we have fought so far, sometimes seems incidental in the light of events in the outside world. We think that once again everything ought to be completely different, that we should leave the whole past behind us and that we should begin all over again. Who can't understand that? But, dear brethren, those of you who have not yet been called up, it is all-important that we do not throw away the grace that God has so far given to us, that we do not despise our office, but learn to live and honour it highly at this very time. We have been called to be preachers of the Gospel and shepherds of the community, and as long as we fulfil this task, God will ask us only one thing: whether faithful service to his community has suffered damage through our fault, whether we have despised the community and the brethren whom he has given to us, if only for a single moment.

We may still preach, and so we should do, as before, with good free consciences. And we should be faithful pastors who do not deny their church even in times of need. We know that God requires this service of us today, and this is the greatest possible service that we can render to men. We do not ask what we may feel like today or tomorrow, but what our task is. So let us not bicker and do each other harm, but be glad and serve.

The texts for 1 September were surprising and promising enough:

'Seek the Lord while he may be found, call upon him while he is near' (Isaiah 55:6)

'Behold, now is the acceptable time; behold now is the day of salvation' (2 Corinthians 6:2)

What does that mean, but that God's hour has struck, it is high time for repentance and prayer, the day of glad tidings has dawned, the harvest of the Word of God will be greater than the harvest of death, victory belongs not to the world but to God? If we really believe that, we and our people will be helped.

We are preachers of justification by grace alone. What must that mean today? It means quite simply that we should no longer equate human ways and aims with divine ways and aims. God is beyond all human plans and actions. Everything must be judged by him. Anyone who evades this judgement of God must die; anyone who subjects himself to it, will live. For to be judged by God is grace which leads to life. He judges in order to have mercy, he humbles in order to exalt. Only the humble will succeed. God does not confirm human action, but cuts across it, and thereby draws our gaze above, to his grace. In cutting across our ways, God comes to us and says his gracious 'Yes' to us, but only through the cross of Jesus Christ. He has placed this cross upon the earth. Under the cross he returns us to the earth, and its work and toil, but in so doing he binds us anew to the earth and to the men who live, act, fight and suffer upon it. 'You then, my son, be strong in the grace that is in Christ Jesus' (2 Timothy 2.1), 'Be strong and show yourself a man, and keep the charge of the Lord your God' (1 Kings 2.2f).

I don't know whether we shall have as troublesome a time now with the question of the righteousness of God as there was in the last war. It almost seems to me as though there had been a change here. Christians today probably know more about the biblical verdict upon the world and history, so they will perhaps be confirmed in their faith, rather than sorely tried by present events. The non-Christians have already finished too completely with the question of the righteousness of a personal God to be overcome with it. Nevertheless, under the pressure of events the question cannot be left completely out of account, on either side, and we shall often have to listen, like the writer of the 42nd Psalm, to the complaint, 'Where is now thy God?' Is it true that God is silent? It is only true for the one whose God is the God of his own ideals and thoughts. He will have to be given the biblical message of the power and fearfulness of the Creator and Lord of the whole world. 'Who has commanded and it came to pass, unless the Lord has ordained it? Is it not from the mouth of the most high that good and evil come?' (Lamentations 3:37f). 'I am the Lord and there is none other, I form light and create darkness, I make weal and create woe' (Isaiah 45:6f), 'Does evil befall a city unless the Lord has done it?' (Amos 3:6).

This God who makes the nations drink from the cup of his wrath and throws them into confusion (Jeremiah 25:15ff), is the Father of our Lord Jesus Christ whose counsel is wonderful and who will carry it our gloriously to the end. (Isaiah 28:29). Is God silent? No, he speaks the silent language of his fearful power and glory, so that we become small and humble and worship him alone. And in pure grace he speaks the clearly perceptible language of his mercy and loving-kindness to the children of men through the mouth of Jesus Christ, in whom we have the omnipotent God for our own father. 'Holy, holy, holy is the Lord of hosts; the whole earth is full of his glory' (Isaiah 6:3).

So our hearts and eyes cannot be caught and dismayed by daily events, however closely we follow them. Above them, we seek and find God the Lord, and in reverence look upon his works. We seek and find our Lord Jesus Christ, and firmly believe in his victory and the glory of his community. We seek and find God, the Holy Spirit, who gives his word power over us, greater power than the world can ever gain over us. And so we pray that the work of the triune God will soon be consummated. Death has again come among us and we must think about it, whether we want to or not. Two things have become important to me recently: death is outside us and it is in us. Death from outside is the fearful foe which comes to us when it will. It is the man with the scythe, under whose stroke the blossoms fall. It guides the bullet that goes home. We can do nothing against it, 'it has power from the supreme God.' It is the death of the whole human race, God's wrath and the end of all life.

But the other is death in us, it is our own death. That too has been in us since the fall of Adam. But it belongs to us. We die daily to it in Jesus Christ, or we deny him. This death in us has something to do with love towards Christ and towards men. We die to it when we love Christ and the brethren from the bottom of our hearts, for love is total surrender to what a man loves. This death is grace and the consummation of love. It should be our prayer that we die this death, that it be sent to us, that death only come to us from outside when we have been made ready for it by this our own death. For our death is really only the way to the perfect love of God.

When fighting and death exercise their wild dominion around us, then we are called to bear witness to God's love and God's peace, not only by word and thought, but also by our deeds. Read James 4.1ff! We should daily ask ourselves where we can bear witness in what we do to the kingdom in which love and peace prevail. The great peace for which we long can only grow again from peace between twos and threes. Let us put an end to all hate, mistrust, envy, disquiet, wherever we can. 'Blessed are the peacemakers, for they shall be called the children of God'.

[*Bonhoeffer's first circular letter of the War.*]'

A CHRISTMAS MESSAGE TO THE BRETHREN

No priest, no theologian stood at the cradle in Bethlehem. And yet all Christian theology has its origin in the wonder of wonders, that God became man. 'Alongside the brilliance of the holy night there burns the fire of the unfathomable mystery of theology.' Sacred theology arises from those who on bended knees do homage to the mystery of the divine child in the stall. Israel had no theology. She did not know God in the flesh. Without the holy night there is no theology. 'God revealed in the flesh', the God-man Jesus Christ, is the holy mystery which theology is appointed to guard. What a mistake it is to think that it is the task of theology to unravel God's mystery, to bring it down to the flat, ordinary human wisdom of experience and reason! It is the task of theology solely to preserve God's wonder as wonder, to understand, to defend, to glorify God's mystery as mystery. This and nothing else was the intention of the ancient Church when it fought with unflagging zeal over the mystery of the persons of the Trinity and the natures of Jesus Christ. How superficial and flippant, especially of theologians, to send theology to the knacker's yard, to make out that one is not a theologian and doesn't want to be, and in so doing to ridicule one's own ministry and ordination and in the end to have, and to advocate, a bad theology instead of a good one! But of course, where in our theological classes were we shown and taught the mystery of God in the flesh, the birth of Jesus Christ, the God-man and Saviour, as the unfathomable mystery of God? Where do we hear it preached? Surely Christmas Eve can kindle in us again something like a love of sacred theology, so that, seized and compelled by the wonder of the cradle of the Son of God, we are moved to consider again, reverently, the mysteries of God. But it may well be that the glow of the divine mysteries has already been quenched, and has died in our hearts as well.

The ancient Church meditated on the question of Christ for many centuries. It imprisoned reason in obedience to Jesus Christ, and in harsh, conflicting sentences gave living witness to the mystery of the person of Jesus Christ. It did not give way to the modern pretence that this mystery could only be felt or experienced, for it knew the corruption and self-deception of all human feeling and experience. Nor, of course, did it think that this mystery could be thought out logically, but by being unafraid to express the ultimate conceptual paradoxes, it bore witness to, and glorified, the mystery as a mystery against all reason.

The Christology of the ancient Church really arose at the cradle of Bethlehem, and the brightness of Christmas lies on its weather-beaten face. Even today, it wins the hearts of all who come to know it. So at Christmas time we should again go to school with the ancient Church and seek to understand in worship what it thought and taught, to glorify and defend belief in Christ. The hard concepts of that time are like stone from which one strikes fire.

Let us look briefly at three well-known christological principles, which survive in our Lutherian Confessions, not only that we might preach them to the congregations, but to put our thought and knowledge, as preachers of the word, to work in the light of holy night.

1. The Fathers were concerned to say that God, the Son, took upon himself *human nature*, not that he took upon himself *a man*. What does that mean? God became man by taking upon himself human nature, not by taking an individual man. This distinction was necessary to preserve the universality of the wonder of Christmas. 'Human nature', that is, the nature, essence, flesh of all human beings, i.e. my nature, my flesh; human nature, that is the embodiment of all human possibilities. Perhaps we moderns might put it more simply by saying that in the birth of Jesus Christ, God took manhood, and not just an individual man. But this taking happened corporeally, and that is the unique wonder of the incarnation. The body of Jesus Christ is our flesh. He bears our flesh. Therefore, where Jesus Christ is, there we are, whether we know it or not; that is true because of the incarnation. What happens to Jesus Christ happens to us. It really is all *our* 'poor flesh and blood' which lies there in the crib; it is *our* flesh which dies with him on the cross and is buried with him. He took human nature so that we might be eternally with him. Where the body of Jesus Christ is, there we are; indeed we are his body. So the Christian message for all people runs: You are accepted, God has not despised you, but he bears in his body all your flesh and blood. Look at the cradle! In the body of the little child, in the incarnate Son of God, your flesh, all your distress, anxiety, temptation, indeed all your sin, is borne, forgiven and healed. If you complain, 'My nature, my whole being is beyond salvation and I must be eternally lost', the Christmas message replies, 'Your nature, your whole being is accepted; Jesus Christ bears it, in this way he has become your saviour.' Because Christmas is the physical acceptance of all human flesh by the gracious God, we must affirm that God's son took human nature upon himself.

2. 'Two natures and one person' — the ancient Church has ventured
to express its knowledge of Christmas in this paradoxical formula.
'Ventured', for it, too, knew that something inexpressible was
expressed here, simply because one could not be silent about it
(Augustine). People found two things in the cradle, and bore witness
to them: manhood taken in the flesh and the eternal Godhead, both
united in the one name of Jesus Christ, human and divine nature
united in the person of the Son of God. Divine nature, that is, the
Godhead: Father, Son and Holy Spirit united for ever. It is the
eternal might, glory and majesty of the triune God. Wherever the
Son is, he brings this divine nature with him, for he remains true
God from eternity to eternity. If the Son of God has truly become
man, the divine nature is certainly also present in all its majesty;
otherwise Christ would not be true God. This really is so: if Jesus
Christ is not true God, how could he *help* us? If Christ is not true
man, how could he help *us*? Of course, the divine nature is hidden in
the cradle, and it shines through the poor rags of the human nature
only here and there in the life of Jesus. But however mysteriously
hidden, it is still present, hidden for us, present for us. Divine and
human nature, united in Christ and still not made one; for otherwise
the vast difference between Godhead and manhood would be done
away with. So it may never be said that the divine nature assumed
the human nature; that would imply that the Father and the Holy
Spirit also took flesh and would thus mean the ultimate confusion of
God and man. No, it means that the Son of God, the divine person
of the Logos, took human nature. But Godhead and manhood,
divine nature and human nature, met and united only in the *person* of
the Son of God, in Jesus Christ. Nowhere else but in and through
the person of Jesus Christ are Godhead and manhood united,
'without confusion, without change, without division, without
separation', as the Chalcedonian definition put it in supreme
paradox, and at the same time in a most reverent preservation of the
mystery of the person of the Mediator. Rarely in later ages has
reason been so ready to humble and surrender itself before the
miracle of God as it does in these words. But precisely because of

that, reason has been made a better instrument for the glorification of the divine revelation. This christological formula, 'Two natures, one person', at the same time has supreme soteriological significance: Godhead and manhood separated from one another before Christ came, united with each other only in the Son of God. Only through the person do the natures have communion with one another, i.e. only through Jesus Christ are Godhead and manhood united.

3. The contribution of the Lutheran Church, added to the ancient Church's christology, consisted in the doctrine of the *genus majestc-ticum* (disputed most vigorously by Reformed theologians) i.e., the doctrine of the mediation of the properties of the divine nature to the human nature which took place in the Incarnation. 'For to make alive, to have all judgement and power in heaven and on earth, to have all things in his hands, to have subjected all things under his feet, to purify from sin, etc., are not created gifts, but divine, infinite properties, which according to the testimony of Scripture are still given and supplied to the *man* Christ' (Formula of Concord, S.D., VII. 55). True, it remains incomprehensible how the human nature, which is our nature, should share the properties of the divine majesty, but this is scriptural doctrine, and it expresses the deepest and ultimate union of God with man thus, so that one can now say with Luther, 'Wherever you can say, "Here is God", you must also say, "So Christ the man is also there". And if you could point to a place where there was God and not man, the person would already be divided. No, friend, where you show me God you must also show me man.' 'It is the glory of our Lord God that he condescends so deeply to the flesh.' Lutheran teaching parried the objection of the Reformed Church that the human nature was no longer taken seriously by referring to the unique miracle, and to Scripture. Indeed, only from this standpoint do we have the right understanding of the Holy Eucharist and the words of the Lord, 'This is my body'. If Christ speaks in this way, then he must know better than any man what the body is and may be. So incarnation and eucharist are

extremely closely connected. The doctrine of the *genus majestaticum* illuminates this connection. The same God who came in the flesh for our salvation gives himself to us with his body and blood in the sacrament. 'The end of the ways of God is bodiliness' (Oetinger).

The thoughts that we have expressed here are ancient ones: they are minute fragments of the edifice of the Church's Christology. But it is not a question of our marvelling at this building, but of our being led by one thought or another to read and consider more reverently and more prayerfully the biblical witness of the mystery of the incarnation of God, and perhaps also to sing Luther's Christmas hymns more thoughtfully and more joyfully.

[*A Christmas circular to the Finkenwalde brethren, to help the young ordinands preach more meaningfully — a practice he continued through the festivals of the Christian year.*][2]

THE RESURRECTION

1. The resurrection of Jesus Christ is God's 'Yes' to Christ and his redeeming work.

The cross was the end, the death of the Son of God, curse and judgement upon all flesh. If the cross were the last word about Jesus, then the world would be lost in death and damnation, without hope, it would have been a victory over God. But God, who alone accomplished salvation for us, raised Christ from the dead. That was the new beginning, which followed the end as a miracle from above, not in accordance with a firm law, as spring follows winter, but because of the incomparable freedom and power of God, which shatters death. 'Scripture has proclaimed how one death devoured the other' (Luther). In this way God has acknowledged Jesus Christ; indeed, as the Apostle can say, the resurrection is the day on which the Son of God is begotten (Acts 13:33; Romans 1:4). The Son receives back his eternal divine glory, the Father has the Son again. So Jesus is confirmed and glorified as the Christ of God which he was from the beginning. In this way, the representative, satisfactory work of Jesus Christ is acknowledged and accepted by God. Jesus uttered his cry of desolation on the cross and then commended himself to the hands of the Father, who was to make what he pleased of him and his work. In the resurrection of Jesus Christ it has become certain that God has said, 'Yes' to his Son and his work. So we hail the Risen One as the Son of God, the Lord and Saviour.

2. The resurrection of Jesus Christ is God's 'Yes' to us.

Christ dies for our sins, he was raised for our justification (Romans 4:25). Christ's death was the death sentence on us and our sins. If Christ had remained dead, this death sentence would still be in force, 'we would still be in our sins' (1 Corinthians 15:17). But because Christ has been raised from the dead, the verdict on us is repealed, and we are risen with Christ (1 Corinthians 15). That is the case because, by virtue of the acceptance of our human nature in the incarnation, we are in Jesus Christ; what happened to him, happens to us for we have been accepted by him. That is no judgement of experience, but a verdict of God, which is to be recognized in faith in God's word.

3. The resurrection of Jesus Christ is God's 'Yes' to all that he has made.

Not destruction, but a re-creation of the body happens here. The body of Jesus emerges from the tomb and the tomb is empty. We cannot see how it is possible, how it is conceivable that the mortal and corruptible body is now the immortal, incorruptible, transfigured body. Nothing is perhaps so clear from the different character of the reports of the encounters of the Risen One with the disciples as the fact that we cannot picture the new body of the Risen One. We know that the body is the same — for the tomb is empty; and that it is a new body — for the tomb is empty. We know that God has judged the first creation and that he has made a new creation like the first. What survives is not an idea about Christ, but the bodily Christ himself. That is God's 'Yes' to the new creature in the midst of the old. In the resurrection we recognize that God has not abandoned the earth, but has taken it back to himself. He has given it a new future, a new promise. The same earth which God created bore the

Son of God and his cross, and on this earth, the Risen One appeared to his own, and to the earth Christ will return on the Last Day. Anyone who affirms the resurrection of Christ can no longer flee the world, nor can he fall victim to the world, for he has recognized the new creation of God in the midst of the old creation.

The resurrection of Jesus Christ demands faith. It is the unanimous testimony of all accounts that the Risen One did not show himself to the world, but only to his own (Acts 10:40ff). Jesus does not display himself to an impartial authority, so as to let the miracle of the resurrection be authenticated before the world, and thus to compel recognition. He means to be believed, preached and believed again. The world sees only the negative side, the earthly expression of the divine wonder. It sees the empty tomb and explains it as the pious mistake of the disciples (Matthew 28:11ff); it sees the joy and hears the messages of the disciples and calls it all visions and auto-suggestion. The world sees the sign, but it does not believe the miracle. Only where the miracle is believed do the signs become divine signs and aids to faith. For the world the empty tomb is an ambiguous *historical* fact, for the faithful it is the *historic* sign of God, who acts in history with men, which necessarily follows from the miracle of the resurrection.

It is impossible to demonstrate the resurrection by historical methods; for the historian, there are only a number of extremely odd facts which are impossible for him to interpret. For example, had the tomb not been empty, it would have been the strongest argument against a physical resurrection and indeed the basis of polemic against Christianity; on the other hand, we never find this objection, but rather the opposition itself confirms the empty tomb (Matthew 28:11), and this is strengthened by the sudden change of circumstances two days after the crucifixion.

Deliberate deception is psychologically excluded by the whole conduct of the disciples before and after, and also by the very inconsistency of the accounts of the resurrection appearances. Self-deception by visions is ruled out as virtually impossible by the unprejudiced historian because of the initial unbelieving, sceptical rejection of the message by the disciples (Luke 24:11, etc.), and also because of the varied character of the appearances. Thus the decision of the historian in this case, which scientifically remains so mysterious, will be dictated by the presuppositions of his particular approach. But in this way it loses interest and importance for a faith which is based upon God's action in history.

So for the world there remains an insoluble riddle, which cannot in any way compel faith in the resurrection of Jesus. But to faith this riddle is a sign of reality, of which one already knows, an impress of the divine action in history. Scholarship can still never prove nor disprove the resurrection of Jesus, for it is a miracle of God. But faith, to which the Risen One shows himself as being alive, recognizes precisely in the testimony of Scripture the historicity of the resurrection as an act of God which in its character as a miracle can present itself to scholarship only as a riddle. The certainty of the resurrection is received only by faith, from present testimony to Christ. It finds its confirmation in this historical impression made by the miracle, as it is reported in Scripture.

It is the grace of Jesus Christ that he still does not reveal himself visibly to the world, for the very moment at which that happened would be the end, and thus the judgement of unbelief. So the Risen One avoids any visible reinstatement before the world; for that would be judgement on the world. He is witnessed to in his community in his hidden glory, and he lets the word bear witness to him before the world, until the Last Day, when he returns visibly to judge all men.

[*The Theological Supplement, March 1940, which was circulated to the younger clergy through the theological commission of the Confessing Church.*][3]

12

CONSPIRATOR AND PASTOR

On 9 September 1940, the State Police Headquarters at Koslin informed me of the National Security Office order IV A 4g 776/40 by which I am prohibited from speaking in public in the territory of the Reich. The reason given is 'disruptive activity'. I reject this charge. In view of my whole attitude, my work and my background, it is unthinkable that I should allow myself to be identified with groups which rightly bear the ignominy of such a charge. I am proud to belong to a family which has for generations earned the gratitude of the German people and state. Amongst my ancestors are General Field-Marshal Count Kalckreuth and the two great German painters of the same name, the church historian Karl von Hase of Jena, well known throughout the academic world of the last century; and the Cauer family, the sculptors. Lieutenant General Graf von der Goltz, who liberated the Baltic, is my uncle, and his son Staatsrat Rüdiger Graf von der Goltz is my first cousin. Lieutenant General von Hase, who is on active service, is also my uncle. For almost thirty years my father has been Ordinarius Professor of Medicine in Berlin, and still holds distinguished public appointments; for centuries his ancestors have been highly respected craftsmen and councillors of what was once the free city of Schwäbisch-Hall, and their portraits are still proudly displayed in the city church there. My brothers and brothers-in-law have senior public appointments; one of my brothers was killed in the World War. It has been the concern of all these men and their families to serve the German state

118

and its people at all times, and to risk their lives in its service. In deliberate affirmation of this spiritual heritage and this inward attitude of my family, I cannot accept the charge of 'disruptive activity'. Any conduct which could be described by this charge is alien to my nature, and is, so far as I am concerned, quite out of the question. My personal work consists predominantly of academic research. I seldom take a public part in church affairs, and then almost always by way of academic theological lectures. So far there has never been any official criticism of anything that I have said. I consider it my task in the German Evangelical Church to see that academic work continues undisturbed and that a high quality of research is maintained, and for my own part to contribute towards keeping German scholarship in high repute.

I have been informed that 'lectures', which I am said to have given to a 'part-time course for theological students', have led to this prohibition. My explanation of this is as follows.

On the occasion of a stay in East Prussia, I was invited to take a Bible study and to give a lecture for a small meeting of Königsberg students of different faculties. Three or four students met at Blöstau, near Königsberg, on 13 July 1940, and there were about as many members of the congregation. In the afternoon I took a Bible study, followed by a short talk about the gospel story of the rich young ruler. I append the outline of the Bible study. On the Sunday morning I conducted worship for the Blöstau congregation and preached on the Gospel for the day. After the service I was sitting and talking for a short time with three or four students when a considerable number of officials of the Secret Police appeared and told us that we must disperse. Our attention was drawn to an order of the end of June 1940, which none of us knew about, as it had never been published, and which was not even produced for us despite our constant requests, according to which the prohibition of part-time meetings for Christian Youth was also to apply to adults of 'Confessional organizations'. One of the officials told me himself that I had nothing more to worry about as they were only carrying out orders as a matter of routine. Another said that they would not have come had they known that there were only four or five people in the group. With this, the meeting ended. What objection could be made to my remarks I do not know. I only know that I dealt exclusively with religious and pastoral questions, which had nothing in the least to do with 'disruptive activity'. Clearly I am available to provide any further information or to discuss the matter. I am also convinced that just a short conversation would make it clear that there is some misunderstanding here and that the charge of an objectionable piece of political conduct on my part cannot be sustained. I could easily explain what I was doing in East Prussia. When I was preaching there in a number of communities, I was helping some pastors who were on active service, so that they would have certainty and assurance that their communities were being cared for in their absence; I also did it to help the communities of the homeland, so that they would not feel neglected during the absence of their pastors. The Secret Police did not make the slightest complaint about any of these sermons.

May I now ask for an opportunity to discuss this, or at least that you should tell me whether I am also to be prevented, through this prohibition, from presenting the results of my wholly non-political activity to small groups? To give an example, may I talk to between twenty and thirty interested hearers about the attitude of Luther to this or that question of Christian belief? I cannot believe that the prohibition is meant to be interpreted in this sense. I therefore ask you to allow me at least this activity. Heil Hitler!

[*A letter of protest at a time when Bonhoeffer was talking with Oster and Dohnanyi about special work with the* Abwehr, *i.e., military intelligence, involved in the Conspiracy.*][1]

LETTERS TO BETHGE FROM THE
BENEDICTINE ABBEY, ETTAL

31 October: Arrived yesterday with a four-hour delay in Münich: a most lively day with a number of people. Today a short visit up here, where I have been invited later on. This evening back to Münich for two more days to meet still more people. It is a most splendid winter up here. I hope you can get here. More soon. . . .

[*Letter written the day after joining the* Abwehr.]

18 November: I've been here since yesterday – a most friendly welcome; eat in the refectory, sleep at the hotel, can use the library, have my own key to the cloister, had a good long chat with the Abbot yesterday, in short, everything one could want. All I need is the desk! Many changes have taken place in my attitude to Catholics over the last six years. . . . Further to my invitation for you to come here I just want to say that I have the best personal contacts with the greatest of the Catholic mission societies (Steyler Mission in Vienna) and that I have had the most pressing invitation to go there. Wouldn't that justify a visit from you? I find the people are open and ready so that I could imagine a fruitful conversation between you. I could take you with me without any difficulty, and I can easily make contact with the Catholic *Volksmission.* I think it would be interesting for you and that it would perhaps be quite opportune to take advantage of something like this. I am not sure how long I shall be here, so come in December! Tell Lokies that I think it important that these contacts should be made now. It would, of course, also be interesting for you here.

21 November: . . . This sort of life isn't strange to me, and I find the regularity and silence very conducive to my work. It would indeed be a loss (and it certainly was a loss at the Reformation) if this form of common life, which has been preserved for fifteen hundred years, should be destroyed, as is thought quite possible here. I think that a great deal of friction, which must inevitably be felt in such a close and permanent life together, is avoided through strict discipline. This provides a very sound basis for work. Some things are really strange, as for instance when historical works are read at lunch and supper in the singing tones of the liturgy; it is sometimes difficult to keep from laughing, particularly if the content is humorous. Otherwise I find the reading in such a large group not at all bad, I also introduced it at the seminary. In the course of time one gets acquainted with all sorts of things. Moreover, the food is excellent. I'm now waiting for Christel and the children . . . a great many people have been called up just now. Why, in the winter?

23 November: I'm glad, despite everything, that you're now so fully occupied. . . . My state of retirement, on the other hand, seems so superfluous; but there's no harm in feeling useless for a while. There's no question about it, at present you are indispensable and that will give you penultimate satisfaction. . . . I sometimes think that my whole business (if it *is* unavoidable) can be a form of cold storage for the future. But of course, how incomparably easy and pleasant our life has been over the past few years, when one considers the burdens which others have borne for years. And what right would I have to quarrel, even for a moment, with my situation, which for others would be a foretaste of paradise! So please do not think that I am abandoning myself without restraint to resignation; I already know and tell myself every morning and every evening what I have to be thankful for. – I've just come from a quite marvellous mass. With Schott in one's hand one can still pray a great deal and be utterly affirmative. It's not simply idolatry, even if I find the way from our own sacrifice for God to God's sacrifice for us, with which the mass is concerned, a hard and apparently very perverse one. But I must learn to understand it better. I'm still a guest over there. The ordered life suits me very well, and I'm surprised at the similarity to much of what we did of our own accord at the seminary. Moreover, the Abbot and a number of the fathers have read my *Life Together*. We're going to discuss it soon. The natural hospitality, which is evidently something specifically Benedictine, the really Christian respect for strangers for Christ's sake, almost makes one ashamed. . .

I'm longing for a eucharist. Recently, by mistake, I went to a Lutheran service of penitence in Münich. But the questions were so fearfully legalistic that I was quite glad not to be invited to the eucharist. It was not much better than a mass! . . . In the peace of my present abode I'm thinking a great deal about the brethren, the Confessing Church, you and your work.

27 November: . . . Today, I've thought of a possible title for my book: 'Preparing the Way and Entering Upon It', corresponding to the two parts of the book (the things before the last and the last things). What do you think of it? But don't bother yourself with questions like that. You've enough to do. . . .
[*This was posthumously incorporated in* Ethics.]

28 November: As I still keep waiting, I want to send you at least a greeting a day. If in the meanwhile it has turned out that you have to leave on Monday (and I suppose from your silence I have to fear the worst), then I can at least be with you by letter. It seems quite unnatural to me not to be able to help you. At the moment all sorts of incidental things are going through my head. . . .

29 November: . . . I will have to travel as soon as possible. How long for, I don't know. An interesting and unique job . . . I still don't know how long you are free, but it is a reprieve and the important thing is that we use it rightly. . . . Now you can still have Advent and Christmas. I shall miss the hymns very much, quite apart from the preaching. I am all the more pleased for you that you can be in Finkenwalde now. I wish you boldness of speech and wisdom, and I shall be with you daily in my thoughts. I don't find it physically easy to stand this hill country. The impenetrability of it sometimes lies like a burden even on one's work. Is *Gebirge* (hill) really connected with *bergen* (hide or shelter)? Sometimes I think so and feel it, but only rarely.

20 January 1941: . . . In my work, I've now come up against the question of euthanasia. The more I come to write, the more I am attracted by the material. I find Catholic ethics in many respects most instructive and more practical than ours. So far it's always been chalked up to them as mere casuistry; today one is thankful for a great deal – and precisely for my present theme. I'm already looking forward very much to the conversations of the next few weeks.

25 January: I'm not leaving until 3 February. Stay in Berlin if you can, at the beginning and middle of March. . . . The reporting business will probably be settled by then – I spoke for quite a while with Justus about Catholic affairs: he will tell you. Nothing new, I would like to get a bit further in March. . . . Yesterday I was with Justus at the opera; Beethoven's *Creatures of Prometheus* as a pantomime. I was not very impressed. The Schiller film, which I saw recently, was very bad; pompous, wordy, unauthentic, badly acted. *Kitsch!* So beware! I thought of Schiller like that when I was in the fourth form.

4 February (Bonhoeffer's birthday): it was splendid at least to be able to exchange a word with you on the telephone. It made one's memories of other birthdays particularly vivid again, and also made one aware that a day like this is really insignificant and unimportant without that morning chorale at my door, which you arranged for me over the years, and without morning and evening prayers together, with personal intercessions. All other, all external signs of love must come into this light, or they lose their splendour. . . . I miss Finkenwalde, Schlönwitz and Sigurdshof more and more. *Life Together* was really my swansong. . . . At the moment, our letters are remarkably the same in content – it confirms that our letters reflect things as they are. You wish me good exciting friends. A man can indeed wish that for himself, and it's a great gift today. Yet the human heart is fashioned in such a way that it doesn't seek the plural, but just the singular, and it rests on that. The demands, the limitations and the riches of a true human relationship are that it touches on the realm of individuality and at the same time essentially depends on faithfulness. There can be individual relationships without faithfulness and there can be faithfulness without individual relationships. Both can be found in the plural. But together (which is rare enough) they look for the singular, and happy is he who has 'succeeded in this great venture'.

It was Gürtner's funeral yesterday. Meiser [Evangelical Bishop of Bavaria] preached – the Catholics refused! Great consternation here at the monastery. The Abbot and Johannes went to the funeral at our request and because of their own convictions. . . . Afterwards, the Abbot went to Faulhaber [Catholic Bishop of Bavaria], who seems to have grown very old! Unfortunately. I'm glad you were able to see Gürtner here. . . .

I still don't have the visa. It must come soon now.

8 February: . . . N. was suddenly taken ill in Münich on Wednesday, and was taken to hospital. The diagnosis is still uncertain (perhaps he brought the illness back from the mission field) and he may perhaps have to have special treatment. I'm very sorry, but of course every conceivable thing is being done. . . .
[*A coded letter – N. is Prelät Neuhäusler; 'taken ill' is arrested; 'hospital' is prison; 'mission field' is hostile attitude to Rome in the Western world; 'special treatment' is concentration camp.*]

10 February: . . . I'm now on the question of marriage (the right of free choice of spouse, marriage laws according to racial or confessional viewpoints, Rome, Nuremberg, sterilization, contraception, etc). Catholic morals are in fact almost intolerably legalistic about all these things. I had a long conversation with the Abbot and Johannes about them. They thought that the attitude of the Church towards contraception was the chief reason why most men no longer come to confession. The practice of confession on this point seems to me to be very dangerous. There is, of course, no absolution without repentance, but what sort of repentance is it that is proved false again every three days? That makes for hypocrisy. In fact, the action is not recognized as sinful, and in that case nothing makes sense. I think that one must allow a great deal of freedom here.

22 February: Today I've made the necessary arrangements. I'm going the day after tomorrow [to Switzerland, under the auspices of the *Abwehr*]. I'll hardly be able to write to you after that. . . .

Good that you were able to discuss with N.N. I think that morally nothing can really be said against suicide; it is a sin of unbelief, but that is no moral disqualification . . . at Gürtner's funeral the Regensburg cathedral choir, to which he himself used to belong, sang, first, 'Lord, let thine angels carry him to Abraham's bosom', then 'O Sacred head'. The 'Though now by insult tortured, all glory be to thee' was especially moving. . . . The family had asked for the hymns. It was the best part of the whole ceremony. In any case, I'm always particularly affected by funerals. The question of what remains in the face of death cannot be avoided on such occasions. That's the time when penitence about uselessness and perseverance especially takes hold of one, and along with it the hope of a life which will stand in the face of death.

I'm still writing to Frau von Kleist . . . the chalices will be consecrated when I leave Ettal. There was general admiration of them, and they were thought to be a wedding present, and great revelations were expected from me. Unfortunately I had to disappoint them . . .

I shall be in Münich again on 24 March. Goodbye.

[*Letters written during the time Bonhoeffer was waiting at Ettal for an assignment from the* Abwehr, *and working on his* Ethics.][2]

DEATH ON ACTIVE SERVICE

Today I must tell you that our brothers Konrad Bojack, F.A. Preuss, Ulrich Nithack and Gerhard Schulze have been killed in the east. . . . Apart from these brothers, who were particularly close to us through our work together, others have been killed: Otto Geogii, brother of Wolf, Martin Franke from Pomerania, Engelke from Brandenburg, Heise from Saxony and Nicholaus from the Rhineland. Some of you will remember from my confirmation class Hans Friedrich von Kleist-Retzow and his brother Jürgen Christoph from Stettin. Both were killed in the east. . . . They have gone before us on the way that we must all tread one day. God reminds those of you who are at the front, in a specially gracious way, to be prepared. We will watch over you with unceasing prayer. Of course, you and all of us will be called by God only at the hour which

God has chosen. Until this hour, which lies in God's hands alone, we will all be preserved, even in supreme danger, and our thankfulness for such preservation should lead us to constantly renewed preparedness.

Who understands the choice of those whom God takes to himself early? Does it not seem to us again and again in the early deaths of Christians as though God were robbing himself of his best instruments at a time when he needed them most? But God makes no mistakes. Does God perhaps need our brothers for some hidden service for us in the heavenly world? We should restrain our human thoughts, which always seek to know more than they can, and keep to what is certain. God has loved anyone whom he has called. 'For his soul was pleasing to the Lord, therefore he took him quickly from the midst of wickedness' (Wisdom 4:14). We know that God and the Devil are locked together in combat over the world, and that the Devil has a word to say even at death. In the face of death we cannot say in a fatalistic way, 'It is God's will'; we must add the opposite, 'It is not God's will'. Death shows that the world is not what it should be, but that it needs redemption. Christ alone overcomes death. Here 'It is God's will' and 'It is not God's will' come to the most acute paradox and balance each other out. God agrees to be involved in something which is not his will, and from now on death must serve God despite itself. From now on, 'It is God's will' also embraces 'It is not God's will'. God's will is the overcoming of death through the death of Jesus Christ. Only in the cross and resurrection of Jesus Christ has death come under God's power and it must serve the purpose of God. Not a fatalistic surrender, but living faith in Jesus Christ, who died and has risen again for us, can seriously make an end of death for us.

In life with Jesus Christ, death as a universal fate which comes to us from outside is contrasted with death from within, one's own death, the free death of dying daily with Jesus Christ. Anyone who lives with Christ dies daily to his own will. Christ in us gives us over to death so that he can live in us. So our inner dying rises up against death from the outside. In this way, the Christian accepts his real death; physical death in the true sense does not become the end, but the consummation of life with Jesus Christ. Here we enter the community of the one who could say at his death, 'It is accomplished'.

Dear brothers, it may be that you now have little time or inclination for such thoughts. There are times in which all reality is so mysterious and oppresses us so much that any direct word seems to destroy the mystery of God for us, that we speak about and would like to hear about the last things only in hints. Everything that we can say about our belief then seems so flat and empty against the reality which we experience and behind which we believe there is an unspeakable mystery. It is the same with you at the front as it is with us at home; whatever is uttered vanishes in a flash, all formulae no longer make contact with reality. There can be something very real in all this, as long as one word does not vanish within us, namely the name of Jesus Christ. That name remains a word, the word around which we gather all our words. In this word alone lies clarity and strength. 'Within my heart abiding, thy name and cross alone my every thought are guiding, to bring me to thy throne.'

Let me end with a request. I know that some of you at the front and here are worried by thoughts about the future of our calling. Let these thoughts rest for a while. So far you have been able to give a good witness for our Church, even to suffer for our brothers. Let us not obscure anything now. We need this bit of earthly light and we shall need it still more. Who can ignore the fact that with this war we have been granted an interval which we really cannot bridge with our thoughts? So we should wait patiently.
[*A circular letter, written to the Finkenwalde brethren on 15 August 1941. Such letters continued until he was arrested.*][3]

JOY IN THE MIDST OF SORROW:
ADVENT SUNDAY, 1942

At the head of a letter which is intended to summon you to joy at a serious hour must stand the names of the brothers who have been killed since last I wrote to you: P. Walde, W. Brandenburg, Hermann

Schroder, R. Lynker, Erwin Shutz, K. Rhode, Alfred Viol, Kurt Onnasch, and in addition to them, many of whom are well known to you, Major von Wedemeyer and his oldest son Max, my former pupil for confirmation.

'With everlasting joy upon their heads . . .' (Isaiah 35:10).

We do not grudge it them; indeed, should we not say that sometimes we envy them in the stillness? Since ancient times, accidie – sorrowfulness of heart, resignation – has been one of the deadly sins. 'Serve the Lord with gladness' (Psalm 100:2) summons us from the Scriptures. This is what our life has been given to us for, what it has been preserved for up to now. Joy belongs, not only to those who have been called home, but also to the living, and no one shall take it from us. We are one with them in this joy, but never in sorrow. How shall we be able to help those who have become joyless and fearful unless we ourselves are supported by courage and joy? I don't mean by this something fabricated, compelled; but something given, free. Joy dwells with God; it descends from him and seizes spirit, soul and body, and where this joy has grasped a man, it grows greater, carries him away, opens closed doors. There is a joy which knows nothing of sorrow, need and anxiety of the heart; it has no duration and it can only drug one for a moment. The joy of God has been through the poverty of the crib and the distress of the cross; therefore it is insuperable, irrefutable. It does not deny the distress where it is, but finds God in the midst of it, indeed precisely there; it does not contest the most grievous sin, but finds forgiveness in just this way; it looks death in the face, yet finds life in death itself. We are concerned with this joy which has overcome the world. It alone is worth believing, it alone helps and heals. The joy of our friends who have been called home is also the joy of those who have overcome – the Risen One bears the marks of the cross upon his body; we are still engaged in conflict daily, they have overcome for all time. God alone knows how near to us or far from us stands the last overcoming, in which our own death can become joy. 'With peace and joy I go hence. . . .' Some of us suffer a great deal from having our senses dulled in the face of all the sorrows which these war years have brought with them. Someone said to me recently, 'I pray every day for my senses not to become dulled'. That is certainly a good prayer. And yet we must be careful not to confuse ourselves with Christ. Christ endured all suffering and all human guilt to the full, indeed he was Christ in that he suffered everything alone. But Christ could suffer alongside men because at the same time he was to redeem them from suffering. He had his power to suffer with men from his love and his power to redeem men. We are not called to burden ourselves with the sorrows of the whole world; in the end, we cannot suffer with men in our own strength because we are unable to redeem them. A suppressed desire to suffer with man in one's own strength must become resignation. We are simply called to look with utter joy on the one who really suffered with men and became their redeemer. We may joyfully believe that there was, there is, a man to whom no human sorrow and no human sin is strange, and who in the profoundest love achieved our redemption. Only in such joy towards Christ, the Redeemer, are we saved from having our senses dulled by the pressure of human sorrow, or from becoming resigned under the experience of suffering.

[*The last circular letter of 1942, his fullest year as a double agent with the* Abwehr.][4]

A RECKONING MADE AFTER TEN YEARS, NEW YEAR 1943

Ten years is a long time in anyone's life. As time is the most valuable thing that we have, because it is the most irrevocable, the thought of any lost time troubles us whenever we look back. Time lost is time in which we have failed to live a full human life, gain experience, learn, create, enjoy and suffer: it is time that has not been filled up, but left empty. These last years have certainly not been like that. . . . One may ask whether there have ever before in human history been people with so little ground under their feet – people to whom every available alternative seemed equally intolerable, repugnant and futile, who looked beyond all these existing alternatives for the source of their strength so entirely in the past or in the future and who yet without being dreamers were able to await the success of their cause so quietly and so confidently. Or perhaps one should rather ask whether the responsible thinking people of any generation that stood at a turning point in history did not feel much as we do, simply because something new was emerging that could not be seen in the existing alternatives.

The great masquerade of evil has played havoc with all our ethical concepts. For evil to appear disguised as light, charity, historical necessity, or social justice is quite bewildering to anyone brought up on our traditional ethical concepts, while for the Christian who bases his life on the Bible it merely confirms the fundamental wickedness of evil. Who stands fast? Only the man whose final standard is not his reason, his principles, his conscience, his freedom or his virtue, but who is ready to sacrifice all this when he is called to obedient and responsible action in faith and in exclusive allegiance to God – the responsible man, who tries to make his whole life an answer to the question and call of God. Where are these responsible people?

Who would deny that in obedience, in their task and calling, the Germans have again and again shown the utmost bravery and self-sacrifice? But the German has kept his freedom by seeking deliverance from self-will through service to the community. Calling and freedom were two sides of the same coin. In this he misjudged the world; he did not realize that his submissiveness and self-sacrifice could be exploited for evil ends. When that happened, the exercise of the calling itself became questionable, and all the moral principles of the Germans were bound to totter. The fact could not be escaped that the German still lacked something fundamental: he could not see the need for free and responsible action, if needs be in opposition to his task and his calling; in its place there appeared on the one hand an irresponsible lack of scruple, and on the other a self-tormenting punctiliousness that never led to action. Civil courage, in fact, can only grow out of the free responsibility of free men. Only now are the Germans beginning to discover the meaning of free responsibility. It depends on God who demands responsible action in a bold venture of faith, and who promises forgiveness and consolation to the man who becomes a sinner in this venture.

Although it is certainly not true that success justifies an evil deed, it is impossible to regard success as something which is ethically quite neutral. Historical success creates a basis for the continuance of life. It is still a moot point whether it is ethically more responsible to take the field, like Don Quixote, against a new age, or to admit one's defeat, accept the new age, and agree to serve it. In the last resort success makes history. . . . As long as goodness is successful, we can afford the luxury of regarding it as having no ethical significance; it is when success is achieved by evil means that the problem arises. . . . We will not and must not be either outraged critics or opportunists, which means giving up the struggle and surrendering to success, but we must take our share of responsibility for the moulding of history in every situation, whether we are the victors or the vanquished. One who will not allow any occurrence whatever to deprive him of his responsibility for the course of history (because he knows that it has been laid on him by God) will thereafter achieve a more fruitful relation to the events of history than that of barren criticism and equally barren opportunism. To talk of going down fighting like heroes in the face of certain defeat is not really heroic at all, but merely a refusal to face the future. The ultimate question for a responsible man to ask is not how he is to extricate himself heroically from the affair, but how the coming generation is to live. It is only from this question, with its responsibility towards history, that fruitful solutions can come, even if for the time being they are very humiliating. In short, it is much easier to see a thing through from the point of view of abstract principle than that of concrete responsibility. The rising generation will always instinctively discern which of these we make the basis of our action, for it is their future which is at stake. . . .

There are people who regard it as frivolous, and some Christians think it impious for anyone to hope and prepare for a better earthly future. They think that the meaning of present events is chaos, disorder and catastrophe; and in resignation or pious escapism they surrender all responsibility for reconstruction and for future generations. It may be that the day of judgement will dawn tomorrow; in that case we shall gladly stop working for a better future, but not before!

In recent years we have become increasingly familiar with death. We surprise ourselves by the calmness with which we hear of the death of one of our contemporaries. We cannot hate it as we used to, for we have discovered some good in it, and have almost come to terms with it. Fundamentally we feel that we really belong to death already, and that every new day is a miracle. It would not be true to say that we welcome death, nor do we try to romanticize death, for life is too great and too precious. Still less do we suppose that danger is the meaning of life – we are not desperate enough for that, and we know too much about the good things that life has to offer, though on the other hand, we are only too familiar with life's anxieties and with all the other destructive effects of prolonged personal insecurity. We still love life, but do not think that death can take us by surprise now. After what we have been through during the war, we hardly dare admit that we should like death to come to us, not accidentally or suddenly through some trivial cause, but in the fullness of life and with everything at stake. It is we ourselves, and not outward circumstances, who make death what it can be, a death freely and voluntarily accepted.

ARE WE STILL OF ANY USE?

We have been silent witnesses of evil deeds; we have been drenched by many storms; we have learnt the art of equivocation and pretence; experience has made us suspicious of others and kept us from being truthful and open; intolerable conflicts have worn us down and even made us cynical. Are we still of any use? What we shall need is not geniuses, or cynics or misanthropes, or clever tacticians, but plain, honest, straightforward men. Will our inward power of resistance be strong enough and our honesty with ourselves remorseless enough, for us to find our way back to simplicity and straightforwardness?

There remains an experience of incomparable value. We have for once learnt to see the great events of world history from below, from the perspective of the outcast, the suspect, the maltreated, the powerless, the oppressed, the reviled – in short from the perspective of those who suffer. The important thing is that neither bitterness nor envy should have gnawed at the heart during this time, that we should have come to look with new eyes at matters great and small, sorrow and joy, strength and weakness, that our perception of generosity, humanity, justice and mercy should have become clearer, freer, less corruptible. We have to learn that personal suffering is a more effective key, a more rewarding principle for exploring the world in thought and action than personal good fortune. This perspective from below must not become the partisan possession of those who are eternally dissatisfied; rather, we must do justice to life in all its dimensions from a higher satisfaction, whose foundation is beyond any talk of 'from below' or 'from above'. This is the way in which we may affirm it.

[*Paragraphs taken from, 'After Ten Years', a Christmas message, 1942, sent to Hans von Dohnanyi, Hans Oster and Eberhard Bethge. One copy was kept under the roof-beams of Bonhoeffer's parents' home in Berlin.*][5]

13

THE PRISONER

[*Bonhoeffer was arrested on 5 April 1943, and charged with 'subversion of the armed forces' on the 29th, Later in the year, Dr Wergin was confirmed as his defence lawyer.*]

LETTER TO HANS VON DOHNANYI,
WHO PERSUADED HIM TO JOIN THE CONSPIRACY:

My dear Hans

Your letter so surprised, delighted and moved me that I could not refrain, at the very least, from attempting to reply to it. Whether this letter reaches you does not lie within my power; but I hope it fervently. For you must know that there is not even an atom of reproach or bitterness in me about what has befallen the two of us. Such things come from God and from him alone, and I know that I am one with you and Christel [his wife, and Bonhoeffer's sister] in believing that before him there can only be subjection, perseverance, patience — and gratitude. So every question, 'Why?' falls silent, because it has found its answer. Until recently, until father's seventy-fifth birthday [when Hitler sent a personal message of congratulation, and honoured him with the Goethe medal for art and science, 31 March 1943], we have been able to enjoy so many good things together that it would be almost presumptuous were we not also ready to accept hardship quietly, bravely — and really gratefully. I know that it is more difficult for you because of Christel and the children; but I know Christel well enough to be troubled only for a moment over her inner disposition; her one wish will be that you do not worry about her. I now want you to know - not to burden you, but simply to delight you and to enable you to share my joy — that since January I have been engaged to Maria von Wedemeyer. Because of the deaths of her father and brother, it was not mentioned until the summer, and I was only to tell my parents. It's a severe trial for Maria, but Mother writes that she is brave, cheerful and confident, so that is a very great encouragement to me. I am convinced that this experience is good for the two of us, even if it is still so incomprehensible. So rejoice with me!

[*Taken from a letter dated, erroneously, 5 April and probably written 5 May 1943.*][1]

LETTERS TO HIS PARENTS ABOUT MARIA:

14 April: . . . As you can imagine, I'm feeling especially sorry for my fiancée at the moment. It's very hard on her, having so recently lost her father and brother in the East. As an army officer's daughter, she may well find the thought of an arrest particularly hard to take. If only I could say a few consoling words to her. Now you will do that for me, and perhaps she'll come to see you in Berlin. That would be wonderful . . .

25 April: . . . It was Maria's birthday on Good Friday. If I didn't know how courageously she bore the death of her father, her brother and two beloved cousins last year, I should be really concerned about her. She'll now have the consolation of Easter and the support of her numerous family, and her Red Cross work will keep her fully occupied. Give her my fond love and tell her that I long to see her again, but that she mustn't be sad, but as brave as she always has been. She's still so young, that's the hard part . . . Incidentally, I'm anxious to know how Maria's grandmother is. If she's dead, please don't keep it from me. Maria and I have both been so attached to her . . . I should be very relieved if Maria could spend a quiet day with you some time.

5 May: I'm delighted that Maria wrote to you in such a courageous and confident vein . . . However fanciful I currently find my secret hope that some time — where? — we shall all celebrate my and

Maria's wedding day together. It's a great and wonderful thought . . . Does everyone know about or engagement by now? It's still in the family though, surely? However, our two 'immediate families' come to more than eighty people, by my reckoning, so I don't suppose it will remain a secret for long . . . What good news that her grandmother is better. She too has a heavy burden to bear, with five of her sons and grandsons killed, and seven still out there. Give her my fond love — I'm sure she's thinking of me![2]

THOUGHTS ON A SCRAP OF PAPER — 8 MAY 1943

Separation from people, from work, the past, the future, from marriage, from God. The various inner attitudes towards the past . . . forgetting . . . the way experiences are cut up — fulfilled, unfulfilled, according to history — self-deception, idealization; concerning the past and concerning the present. A sober view of things instead of illusions — the disappearance of memories, self-pity [in English]; for the one who has overcome; humour. Passing, killing time. Smoking in the emptiness of time. Remembering the possible, although non-concrete. The significance of illusion.
[*Then on the back of the scrap paper:*]
The experience of the past, fulfilment, thanks, penitence — the feeling of time — not only the present results . . . Waiting — but, for example, facing death quite calmly — the peasant's time, but no sense of 'time' itself — the experience of time as the experience of separation, engaged couples, from God — past. Why 'In a hundred years all over' and not: when we have known good fortune until recently. No possession that outlasts time, no task — Flight from the experience of time in dreams, the shock of awakening. Also in dreams, the past means the future, dreams are timeless. — Tooth of time, i.e. gnawing time — also healing time, like the healing of a wound.[3]

THE WEDDING SERMON FROM A PRISON CELL - MAY 1943

It is right and proper for a bride and bridegroom to welcome and celebrate their wedding day with a unique sense of triumph. When all the difficulties, obstacles, hindrances, doubts and misgivings have been, not made light of, but honestly faced and overcome — and it is certainly better not to take everything for granted — then both parties have indeed achieved the most important triumph in their lives. With the 'Yes' that they have said to each other, they have by their free choice given a new direction to their lives; they have cheerfully and confidently defied all the uncertainties and hesitations with which, as they know, a lifelong partnership between two people is faced; and by their own free and responsible action they have conquered a new land to live in. Every wedding must be an occasion of joy that human beings can do such great things, that they have been given such immense freedom and power to take the helm of their life's journey. The children of the earth are rightly proud of being allowed to take a hand in shaping their own destinies, and something of this pride must contribute to the happiness of bride and bridegroom.

We ought not to be in too much of a hurry here to speak piously of God's will and guidance. It is obvious, and it should not be ignored, that it is your own very human wills that are at work here, celebrating their triumph; the course that you are taking at the outset is one that you have chosen for yourselves; what you have done and are doing is not, in the first place, something religious, but something quite secular. So you yourselves, and you alone, bear responsibility for what no one can take from you; or, to put it more exactly, you, Eberhard, have all the responsibility for the success of your venture, with all happiness that such responsibility involves, and you, Renate, will help your husband and make it easy for him to bear that responsibility, and find your happiness in that. Unless you can boldly say today: 'That is *our* resolve, *our* love, *our* way', you are taking refuge in a false piety. 'Iron and steel may pass away, but *our* love shall abide for ever.' That desire for earthly bliss, which you want to find in one another, and in which, to quote the medieval song, 'one is the comfort of the other in body and soul' — that desire is justified before God and man.

Certainly you two, of all people, have every reason to look back with thankfulness on your lives up to now. The beautiful things and joys of life have been showered upon you, you have succeeded in everything, and you have been surrounded by love and friendship. Your ways have, for the most part, been smoothed before you took them, and you have always been able to count on the support of your families and friends. Everyone has wished you well, and now it has been given to you to find each other and to reach the goal of your desires. You yourselves know that no one can create and assume such a life from his own strength, but that what is given to one is withheld from another; and that is what we call God's guidance. So today, however much you rejoice that you have reached your goal, you will be just as thankful that God's will and God's way have brought you here; and however confidently you accept responsibility for your action today, you may and will put it today with equal confidence into God's hands.

As God today adds his 'Yes' to your 'Yes', as he confirms your will with his will, and as he allows you, and approves of your triumphs and rejoicing and pride, he makes you at the same time instruments of his will and purpose, both for yourselves and for others. In his unfathomable condescension God does add his 'Yes' to yours; but by so doing, he creates out of your love something quite new — the holy estate of matrimony.

[*Bonhoeffer expounds five statements:*]

 God is guiding your marriage
 God makes your marriage indissoluble
 God establishes a rule of life by which you can live together
  in wedlock
 God has laid on marriage a blessing and a burden
 God gives you Christ as the foundation of your marriage

[*He then concludes:*]

From the first day of your wedding till the last the rule must be: 'Welcome one another . . . for the glory of God.' That is God's word for your marriage. Thank him for it; thank him for leading you thus far; ask him to establish your marriage, to confirm it, to sanctify it, and preserve it. So your marriage will be 'for the praise of his glory'. Amen..

[*Sent from prison on the occasion of the marriage of Eberhard Bethge to his niece, Renate Schleicher.*][4]

THE EFFECT OF PRISON LIFE

Time is not of much account here. I'm glad the weather is mild. A little while ago a tomtit had its nest, with its ten little ones, in a recess in the yard here. I enjoyed going to look at it every day until some cruel fellow went and destroyed the lot and left some of the tomtits lying on the ground, dead; I can't understand it. When I walk in the yard I get a great deal of pleasure from a small ant-hill and from the bees in the limetrees. I sometimes think of the story of Peter Bamm, who was on a lovely island where he met all kinds of people, good and bad. He dreamt in a nightmare that a bomb might come and destroy everything, and the first thing that occurred to him was, what a pity it would be for the butterflies! Prison life brings home to one how nature carries on uninterruptedly its quiet, open life, and it gives one quite a special – perhaps a sentimental – attitude towards animal and plant life, except that my attitude towards the flies in my cell remains very unsentimental! In general, a prisoner is no doubt inclined to make up, through an exaggerated sentimentality, for the soullessness and lack of warmth in his surroundings; and perhaps he may react too strongly to anything sentimental that affects him personally. The right thing for him to do then is to call himself to order with a cold shower of common sense and humour, to avoid losing his sense of proportion. I believe it is just here that Christianity, rightly understood, can help particularly. You, father, know all this quite well from your long experience of prisoners. I am not yet sure what the so-called prison psychosis is, though I am getting a pretty good idea.

[*From a letter to his parents, 24 June 1943.*][5]

THE CELL-BOUND EXISTENCE

It would be so much better if I could write to you in such a way as to express nothing but my gratitude, joy and happiness at having you, and without conveying any hint of the stress and impatience occa-

sioned by my long cell-bound existence. But that would not be wholly sincere, and it would strike me as unfair to you. I'm sure you're aware of my true state of mind and don't regard me as a born pillar saint. For my part, I can't conceive of your wanting to marry such a man — nor, from my knowledge of ecclesiastical history, would I recommend it. So to set the scene for you: it's 30° [Celsius], I've just had some hot gruel for supper, and I'm sitting at the desk with my sleeves rolled and my collar open, thinking longingly of you. I'd like to drive through the woods with you to the lakeside, go swimming and lie in some shady spot with you, listening to you for ages without saying a word. My desires are thoroughly natural and concrete, as you see, and I'm temporarily giving free rein to an equally natural dislike of my present state. The sun has always attracted me, and I've often been reminded by it that human beings were taken from the earth and don't just consist of thin air and thoughts. So much so once, when I went to Cuba to preach there at Christmas and exchanged the ice of North America for its luxuriant tropical vegetation, I almost succumbed to sun-worship and could hardly remember what I was really supposed to preach. It was a genuine crisis, and a hint of it assails me every summer when I get to feel the sun. To me the sun isn't an astronomical magnitude but a kind of vital force which I love and also fear. I think it's so cowardly to disregard these realities in a rationalistic way. Do you understand? That's why patience and joy and gratitude and serenity and forgiveness must keep fighting and prevailing over all forms of opposition; and really to perceive and learn and believe what it says in the Psalm — 'The Lord God is a sun and a shield' — is something reserved for moments of merciful exaltation, not a conventional wisdom.
[*From a letter to Maria, 20 August 1943.*][6]

WAITING FOR TRIAL

About my request for a lawyer to defend me, I very much hope that this has not caused you any great anxiety, but that you are waiting, as I am, for things to take their course. You really mustn't imagine that I am uneasy or depressed. Of course, this has been a disappointment for me, as I suppose it has been for you too. But in a way I feel freer now that I know my case will soon be finally cleared up, after we have been kept waiting for so long. I'm expecting more information every day.

It doesn't matter if Rüdiger Goltz cannot now make himself available so quickly. Dr Roeder expressed the opinion that it is a case that any decent lawyer can cope with, and if he's a competent, warm-hearted respectable man who also can argue quietly and with distinction, keeping the tone that has so far been maintained in the proceedings — and you can best judge that — I am fully in agreement. Personally, I really have the feeling that one best says oneself what one has to say; but for legal matters, which I do not understand, I imagine that a lawyer is necessary.

[*From a letter to his parents, 3 August 1943.*]¹

14

MARIA VON WEDEMEYER

(*Extracts from Bonhoeffer's letters*)

THE EFFECT OF A VISIT

How can I convey to you what your visits mean to me? They dispel every shadow and every heart ache and remain a day-long source of great serene happiness — and if you knew how much that means to a prisoner you would also know that nothing could be more important. That I need not torment myself when thinking of you, that my longing to be with you need not distress me in any way, but that I can think of you and long for you with quiet confidence and joy — that is what I owe to you, to your dear brave heart and your love. I'm very, very grateful that, for my sake, you requested — and were permitted to request — a visit at such an unusual hour. When I return to my cell after being with you, my prevailing emotion is not, as you may possibly suppose, one of despair at my captivity; no, I'm overwhelmed by the thought that you accepted me. There are so many understandable reasons why you could have said no, but you said yes in spite of them all, and I seem to sense that you say it with ever greater freedom and assurance. In view of that, all the bars over my window melt away and you are with me. Why should I care about the locked door? . .

If thoughts of the loyalty and love of so many friends have restored my courage during spells of fruitless self-criticism in the past, I now feel, more and more, that you and your willingness to become my wife will enable me to face life with confidence of an entirely new order. And whenever I see you again for an hour, I know I can never lose that confidence. If that is so now, think how it will be when we are really together!
[*27 August 1943*][1]

ANTICIPATION OF MARRIAGE

I'm so glad you're not in Berlin now. It makes the air-raid nights easier and your 34-strong household must be giving you plenty to do. Besides, it's very reassuring to know you're busy with your trousseau. I picture that in every detail and in full colour, and I'm glad of it, it's such an image of calm, confidence and happiness. When shall I see and admire and delight in all those things? And when shall we use them together in our daily life and, at the same time, recall the strange times in which they originated? It can't be very much longer. But we'll be patient to the last and look upon this difficult time of waiting, too, as God's way with us, until one day, perhaps, we gain a better understanding of why it was good for us. My dearest Maria, you can't know what it means to me to be at one with you in this. How strange your path through life must often seem to you these days. But one has to climb a mountain, too, in zigzags, or one would never reach the top, and from up there one can often see quite clearly why such a route was necessary.

Some time read Gottfried Arnold's hymn, a very special favourite of mine, though few people know it. The text and tune are difficult, almost too difficult for a congregational hymn, but it grows on one. It begins, 'So führst Du doch . . .' ('Right gladly, Lord, thou leadest thus thy people') and its in the hymnbook.
[9 September 1943][2]

'SEASONS OF MIST AND MELLOW FRUITFULNESS'

Autumn begins tomorrow. These last few weeks, whenever people have spoken of autumn coming early, I've disliked the sound of the word. The changing seasons are harder on us in here than outside. You'll now be spending a lot of time in the forest hides at dusk and before daybreak. I'm so fond of those autumn mornings when the sun breaks slowly through the mist, but I know that, wherever you are, you'll be waiting with me every day and every hour. This is turning into a wait whose outward purpose I fail to understand, and whose inward purpose has to be rediscovered daily. The last few months have deprived us both of a great deal. Time is today's most precious commodity, for who can tell how much more of it a person has been granted? Yet I refuse to believe that our past and present separation is time lost, either for each of us individually or both together. We have grown together in a way that differs from our expectations and desires, but there are, and will doubtless continue to be, other times when all will ultimately depend on our being of one mind and sticking together. Your life would have been very different — easier, simpler, more predictable — had our paths not crossed a year ago, but I'm only troubled by that thought for a brief moment. I believe that you, as well as I, had reached a stage in life at which our meeting was inevitable. Neither of us had any fundamental desire for an easy life, much as we can both take pleasure in life's lovely, happy times, and much as we doubtless yearn for such times today. For both of us, I believe, happiness lies elsewhere, in a more remote place that not only passes many people's understanding but will continue to do so. At bottom, we both seek tasks to perform. Each of us has hitherto sought them separately, but from now on, they'll be common tasks in which we shall fully grow together — if God grants us the requisite time. [*20 September 1943*][3]

A VISIT AND RAINER MARIA RILKE

Yesterday your visit and your parcel, today your letter — I almost feel that little more is needed to make my happiness complete! There was only one thing wrong with the visit; it happened so suddenly in spite of my long wait — I was informed of it only two minutes beforehand — that anticipation was denied its due! . . . Nice though it is that they've exempted us from the gloomy atmosphere of those frightful little booths, that sofa always makes me feel as if I'm in the front row in class and expected to behave!

And now to your Rilke. Thank you for sending it. I already knew those letters, but I've reread them with pleasure, thinking of you. But, as you already know, I'm somehow on a different wavelength and have always wondered while reading them how one should view such letters, which were (or so I assume and hope!) originally intended to be

purely personal. I can't simply accept them as applying to myself, and I believe it would be a mistake to be seduced into doing so by their beauty of thought and language, still less to arrange one's life accordingly. Rilke would surely have written in a very different vein to me — and I believe to you (though I'm positive that in my case he wouldn't have done so at all!). To employ a musical analogy, I always have to transpose Rilke from D flat major to C major for my benefit, and there are times when I wouldn't observe his pianissimo — nor would you! Forgive me for saying all this, but I feel that it somehow possesses more than mere literary relevance. We must discuss this further some time.
[*8 October 1943*][4]

'PAIN IS A HOLY ANGEL'

Today is *Totensonntag* [the day when Protestants in Germany remember their dead — the Sunday before Advent] so you'll all be together in church and near the crosses. Stifter once put it very beautifully: 'Pain is the holiest angel who reveals treasures that would otherwise have remained hidden in the depths for ever. People have become greater through it than through all the world's joys.' It is so, as I keep telling myself in my present predicament: the pain of deprivation, which is often physically perceptible, must exist, and we should not and need not argue it away. But it has to be overcome anew every time, so there is an even holier angel than pain, and that is joy in God. By the time you receive this letter it will probably be Advent, a time especially dear to me. A prison cell like this, in which one watches and hopes and performs this or that ultimately insignificant task, and in which one is wholly dependent on the door's being opened from outside, is a far from inappropriate metaphor for Advent.
[*21 November 1943*][5]

THE FIRST CHRISTMAS IN PRISON

Without abandoning all hope that things may yet take a turn for the better just in time, I must now write you a Christmas letter. Be brave, dearest Maria, even if this letter is the only token of my love this Christmas. We shall both experience a few dark hours — why

should we disguise that from each other? We shall ponder the incomprehensibility of our lot and be assailed by the question of why, over and above the darkness already enshrouding humanity, we should be subjected to the bitter anguish of a separation whose purpose we fail to understand. How hard it is, inwardly to accept what defies our understanding; how great is the temptation to feel ourselves at the mercy of blind chance; how sinister the way mistrust and resentment steal into our hearts at such times; and how readily we fall prey to the childish notion that the course of our lives reposes in human hands! And then, just when everything is bearing down on us to such an extent that we can scarcely withstand it, the Christmas message comes to tell us that all our ideas are wrong, and that what we take to be evil and dark is really good and light because it comes from God. Our eyes are at fault, that is all. God is in the manger, wealth in poverty, light in darkness, succour in abandonment. No evil can befall us; whatever men may do to us, they cannot but serve the God who is secretly revealed as love and rules the world and our lives. We must learn to say: 'I know how to be abased and I know how to abound; in any and all circumstances I have learnt the secret of facing plenty, and hunger, abundance and want. I can do all things in him who strengthens me' (Philippians 4:12, 13) — and this Christmas in particular can help us to do so. What is meant here is not stoical resistance to all extraneous occurrences, but true endurance and true rejoicing in the knowledge that Christ is with us . . . let us celebrate Christmas in this way. Be as happy with the others as a person can only be at Christmas time. Don't entertain any awful imaginings of me in my cell, but remember Christ also frequents prisons, and that he will not pass me by. Besides, I hope to find myself a good book for Christmas and read it in peace!
[13 December 1943][6]

A MAJOR HEARTACHE

Your mother was here yesterday. We had a good talk and I am immensely grateful to her, but I have to write you this letter to get over my first really major heartache of the past year . . . Mother told me that you're somehow not entirely satisfied with your visits here. She proposed, obviously at Grandmother's suggestion, that I treat you to a brief biblical exegesis each time, in other words that we hold a little prayer meeting together. She said you should come prepared with questions for us to discuss. Well Maria, the whole idea is impossible, and I would find it alien and unnatural. We shouldn't 'make' something of our brief moments together — no, that's out. So far from wanting something ultra-special, great and important from you during your visits — after all, we both know what we do each night and morning! — I simply want you as you are in reality, without effort or deliberation. That's 'greater' and far more 'important' than any 'importance' or 'greatness', because it's real life, just as it flows from the hand of God. Some visits are better than others, granted, but isn't life itself like that, and isn't the main requirement that we are together in the way we are now and mean to live together later on? Dear Maria, if despair and doubt become too much for you, write to me yourself! How could I say even to Mother — with a prize gossip sitting in on our conversation — what I would hesitate to tell even you, because important matters should be reserved for important occasions? I understand Mother so well and am so glad you've had her this past year, but I neither can nor should tell anyone else what I want to tell you. It belongs to us alone, just you and me. Grandmother once called me 'reticent', and I'm afraid that once voiced, such characterizations stick. What Grandmother means by 'reticence' is that I don't discuss everything, nor do I wish to, even with my intimates. For all the love I bear my parents and brothers and sisters, and for all my close friendship with Grandmother, there are certain things I do not discuss with them because they're incompatible with the nature of our relationship. Grandmother dislikes that, but she can't, I fear, change it because I consider it the right and proper thing for me personally. I don't believe that the people who really know me think me reticent, and I'm sure, dearest Maria, that one day you'll marvel at how un-reticent I am — indeed how immensely difficult I shall find it to keep things to myself, and how I long to share with you what I withhold from others. Most people think me quiet, aloof, even forbidding; you will come to know a different side of me. Grandmother evidently believes that I somehow expect something more from you during our meetings. She couldn't be more mistaken, and I can only marvel at how little she knows me in that respect. As if I am forever eager to engage in profound, intellectual discussions! It's precisely because I am already so certain of our agreement on fundamentals that we've no need to discuss the mysteries of existence all the time, but can take things as they come and continually rediscover each other in the ordinary things of life. There will be times when we are drawn to fundamentals of our own accord, but God subsists not only in fundamentals but in every day life as well.

[*11 March 1944*][7]

ON HER TWENTIETH BIRTHDAY

. . . You're twenty years old. I'm thoroughly ashamed to recall how ignorant I was at that age, and how replete your own life already is, by comparison with experiences and tasks of the utmost importance. I still believed then that life consisted of ideas and books, and wrote my first book, and was, I'm afraid to say, inordinately proud of it. But what did I give anyone at that stage? Whom did I help? Whom did I make glad and happy? What did I really know of the things I wrote about? And you? You don't write books, fortunately; you do, know, learn, and fill with real life that which I have only dreamed of. Perception, coalition, emotion and suffering don't disintegrate in your case; they're a grand totality of which one constituent reinforces and complements the other. You yourself don't realize that, and it's much the best that way — so forget it and always remain as you are . . .

[*16 April 1944*][8]

HOLY WEEK AND FREEDOM IN CHRIST

... I was very moved and exercised by what you wrote about your Holy Week. I'm glad you told me everything, including Stählin's unpleasant remark [to Hesi von Truchsees, 'Why not send Maria away, she needn't take part in Holy Week. If I know her, she won't be able to endure having to choose between her father and her fiancé, and it'll be impossible to avoid that decision after a Holy Week']. He shouldn't have made that remark, and he can hardly hope to justify it. Where lies the fanaticism for which we're so fiercely vilified, on his side or mine? I'm very sorry that he should have strayed so far from the Christian spirit; it must stem from great resentment of the Confessing Church, which itself may be partly to blame, albeit only where its immature representatives are concerned. No, dearest Maria, you've no need to choose between your father and me . . . I firmly believe that Father and I would always have regarded each other as brothers in Christ, even if we had differed on this point or that, and may even have thought each other mistaken in some respects. We would always have been quite prepared to learn from each other, certainly, and would have only wished to assist each other in the knowledge of Christ and in his love — especially at a time like the present, when all that matters is whether or not one opts for Christ, not Christian opinion. I'm all in favour of unequivocal decisions when they are needed, but it's wrong — for God's sake — in this age of necessary decisions to bully people into making decisions which are neither genuine nor necessary! I'm glad that Holy Week reinforced your belief in Christ, which would also imply that you don't allow yourself to be influenced, either by people or by considerations of taste. However sure it is that no one owes one's faith to certain people, every Christian should be *sui juris* (one's own judge) and obedient solely to God and his word, not to other people and their ideas. Faith and style are mutually exclusive. My chief quarrel with the *Berneucheners* [a high church Lutheran movement, largely in north Germany] is that they saddle the Christian faith with a style, and thus prevent people from attaining full freedom under the word of God . . . I'm very grateful to the *Berneucheners* for the witness to Christ which they share, but I oppose all forms of stylization. I wish to be a Christian and a free person, not a Christian and a *Berneuchener*, and in that respect I wish very much that we were of one mind. If, during Holy Week, you had heard nothing, *absolutely nothing*, but the Gospel of Christ, you would probably have been guided towards certainty, joy and clarity, not burdened with doubts and problems. I am not, of course, claiming that I could preach Christ without human adjuncts; but I try, and have always tried, to guide people to complete freedom under the Word and not to bind them to myself — however often I may have failed in that endeavour. So don't brood about Holy Week, but take from it whatever leads you to freedom under Christ. Disregard everything else, and always do the same when you hear me preach, and tell me whenever you hear me lay down alien laws and speak with alien voices. We want to obey and belong to Christ, no one else!

You recently wrote that the good things of the past avail us little once they're over. I myself have often wrestled with that idea, during the past year in particular and especially in the beginning, but I've discovered that it is very dangerous and wrong, and that one mustn't yield to it. We mustn't lose our past. It belongs to us and must remain a part of us, otherwise we grow discontented or depressed. We must continually bathe all that is past in a solution of gratitude and penitence; then we shall gain and preserve it. It is the past, granted, but it is *my* past and as such it will retain its immediacy if we are profoundly, unselfishly grateful for God's gifts and regretful for the perverse way in which we so often vitiate them. That is how, without tormenting ourselves, we can look back on the past and draw on all its strength. God's grace and God's forgiveness preside over all that is past.

[*Smuggled letter, undated, written at the end of April 1944.*][9]

THE PAST

You went, beloved happiness and much-loved sorrow.
What shall I call you? Mercy, life, bliss,
part of myself, my heart — the past?
The door slammed shut;
I hear footsteps slowly recede and die away.
What is there left for me? Joy? Anguish? Desire?
This only do I know: you went — and all is gone.

Do you feel how I now reach out for you,
clinging so tightly that I cannot fail to hurt you,
how I rend you till the blood flows,
just to be sure that you are near,
you full, corporeal, earthly life?
Do you sense that I now desire pain
of my own,
that I crave to see my own blood,
lest everything subside — in the past?

Life, what have you done to me?
Why did you come? Why did you slip away?
Past, though you flee from me,
do you not remain my past, my own?

Just as the sun sinks ever faster over the sea
as if drawn down into darkness,
so sinks and sinks and sinks
unceasingly
your image into the sea that is the past,
and is buried beneath a wave or two.

Just as a puff of warm breath
dissolves in cool morning air,
so does your image melt away
until I see your face, your hands, your form
no more.
A smile, a glance, a word comes back to me,
but all disintegrates,
dissolves,
is desolate and remote,
is destroyed,
is solely in the past.

I yearn to inhale the fragrance of your being,
absorb and linger therein,
just as, on a hot summer's day,

heady blossoms make bees welcome
and intoxicate them,
and as hawkmoths become drunk on privet.
But a rude gust scatters scent and blossoms,
and I stand there like a fool
before the vanished and the bygone.

I feel as if, with fiery pincers, fragments have been torn
from my flesh
when you, my bygone life, hurry away.
Assailed by fury and defiance
I ask wild futile questions,
forever saying, Why, why, why?
If my senses cannot hold you back,
life that is fleeting and has flown,
I shall think and think again
until I find what I have lost.
But I sense
that all above, beside, below me
is smiling at me, mysterious and intact,
smiling at my hopeless endeavour
to capture the wind
and regain what is past.
My eyes and soul grow angry;
I hate what I see,
hate what moves me,
hate everything alive and beautiful
that would requite me for my loss.
I want my life, I demand my own life
back again
my past — you!

You — a tear springs to my eye —
can it be that through a veil of tears
I shall regain
your whole image,

you in your entirety?
But I'll not weep.
Tears avail the strong alone;
the weak, they sicken.

The evening finds me weary.
Welcome is the bed
that promises forgetfulness
if possession be denied me.
Extinguish, Night, what burns in me,
grant me complete oblivion,
be charitable to me, Night, fulfil your kindly function,
to you I entrust myself.
But Night is wise and strong,
wiser than I and stronger than Day.
That which no earthly power can accomplish,
that on which thoughts and senses, defiance and tears
cannot but founder,
Night bestows upon me in abundance.
Unscathed by hostile time, pure, free and whole,
you are brought to me in dreams:
you, the past; you, my life;
you, yesterday; yesterday's hour.

Your nearness awakens and alarms me
at dead of night.
Have I lost you once more? Am I always to seek you
in vain,
you, my past, my own?
I stretch forth my hands
and pray,
and hear the new tidings:
The past will be restored to you,
as your life's most vital part,
by gratitude and penitence.
Take hold, in what is past,

of God's forgiveness and grace.
Pray that God may preserve you,
today and on the morrow.[10]

LETTER ACCOMPANYING THE POEM, 'THE PAST'

This is for you and you alone. I hesitated to send it because I was afraid it might alarm you. It mustn't, nor will it, I think, if you sense what underlies it. The last six lines are what matters most, and they prompted all the rest. I hold fast to them, and so do you! I can't write any more today. Everything I could say is in my poem. If you don't like it, tear it up and throw it away. But I didn't want to conceal it from you.

[*Bonhoeffer had sent the first version of this poem to Eberhard Bethge and amended it with several minor alterations before sending the above version to Maria.*][11]

15

EBERHARD BETHGE
(*EXTRACTS FROM*
BONHOEFFER'S LETTERS)

THE BAPTISM OF EBERHARD'S FIRST CHILD
(*ADDRESSED TO THE CHILD*)

Today you will be baptized a Christian. All those great ancient words of the Christian proclamation will be spoken over you, and the command of Jesus Christ to baptize will be carried out on you, without your knowing anything about it. But we are once again being driven right back to the beginnings of our understanding. Reconciliation and redemption, regeneration and the Holy Spirit, love of our enemies, cross and resurrection, life in Christ and Christian discipleship – all these things are so difficult and so remote that we hardly venture any more to speak of them. In the traditional words and acts we suspect there may be something quite new and revolutionary, though we cannot as yet grasp or express it. That is our fault. Our Church, which has been fighting in these years only for its self-preservation, as though that were an end in itself, is incapable of taking the word of reconciliation and redemption to mankind and the world. Our earlier words are therefore bound to lose their force and cease, and our being Christians today will be limited to two things: prayer and righteous action among men. All Christian thinking, speaking and organizing must be born anew out of this prayer and action. By the time you have grown up, the Church's form will have changed greatly. We are not yet out of the melting-pot, and any attempt to help the church prematurely to a new expansion of its organization will merely delay its conversion and purification. It is not for us to prophesy the day (though the day will come) when men will once more be called so to utter the Word of

God that the world will be changed and renewed by it. It will be a new language, perhaps quite non-religious, but liberating and redeeming – as was Jesus' language; it will shock people and yet overcome them with its power, it will be the language of a new right-eousness and truth.

[*Bonhoeffer was unable to attend the baptism, but sent his 'sermon'; May 1944.*][1]

WORLD COME OF AGE

You now ask so many important questions on the subjects that have been occupying me lately, that I should be happy if I could answer them myself. But it's all very much in the early stages; and as usual, I'm being led on more by an instinctive feeling for questions that will arise later than by any conclusions that I've already reached about them. I'll try to define my position from the historical angle.

The movement that began about the thirteenth century towards the autonomy of man (in which I would include the discovery of the laws by which the world lives and deals with itself in science, social and political matters, art, ethics and religion) has in our time reached an undoubted completion. Man has learnt to deal with himself in all questions of importance without recourse to the 'working hypothesis' called 'God'. In questions of science, art and ethics this has become an understood thing at which one now hardly dares to tilt. But for the last hundred years it has also become increasingly true of religious questions; it is becoming evident that everything gets along without 'God' – and, in fact, just as well as before. As in the scientific field, so in human affairs generally, 'God' is being pushed more and more out of life, losing more and more ground.

Roman Catholic and Protestant historians agree that it is in this development that the great defection from God, from Christ, is to be seen; and the more they claim and play off God and Christ against it, the more the development considers itself to be anti-Christian. The world that has become conscious of itself and the laws that govern its own existence has grown self-confident in what seems to us to be an uncanny way. False developments and failures do not make the world doubt the necessity of the course that it is taking, or of its development; they are accepted with fortitude and detachment as part of the bargain, and even an event like the present war is no exception. Christian apologetics has taken the most varied forms of opposition to this self-assurance. Efforts are made to prove to a world thus come of age that it cannot live without the tutelage of 'God'. Even though there has been surrender on all secular problems, there still remain the so-called 'ultimate questions' – death, guilt – to which only 'God' can give an answer, and because of which we need God and the Church and the pastor. So we live, in some degree, on these so-called ultimate questions of humanity. But what if one day they no longer exist as such, if they too can be answered 'without God'? Of course, we now have the secularized offshoots of Christian theology, namely existentialist philosophy, and the psychotherapists, who demonstrate to secure, contented and happy mankind that it is really unhappy and desperate and simply unwilling to admit that it is in a predicament about which it knows nothing, and from which only they can rescue it. Wherever there is health, strength, security, simplicity, they scent luscious fruit to gnaw at or to lay their pernicious eggs in. They set themselves to drive people to inward despair, and then the game is in their hands. That is secularized methodism. And whom does it touch? A small number of intellectuals, of degenerates, of people who regard themselves as the most important thing in the world, and who therefore like to busy themselves with themselves. The ordinary man, who spends his life at work and with his family, and of course with all kinds of diversions, is not affected. He has neither the time nor the inclination to concern himself with his existential despair, or to regard his perhaps modest share of happiness as a trial, a trouble or a calamity.

The attack by the Christian apologetic on the adulthood of the world I regard as in the first place, pointless; in the second place, ignoble; and in the third place, unChristian. Pointless, because it seems to me like an attempt to put a grown-up man back into adolescence, i.e., to make him dependent on things, on which he is, in fact, no longer dependent, and thrusting him into problems which are, in fact, no longer problems to him. Ignoble, because it amounts to an attempt to exploit man's weakness for purposes that are alien to him and to which he has not freely assented. UnChristian because it confuses Christ with one particular stage in man's religiousness, i.e., with human law. More about this, later. But first, a little more about the historical position. The question is: Christ and the world that has come of age. The weakness of liberal theology was that it conceded to the world the right to determine Christ's place in the world; in the conflict between the Church and the world it accepted the comparatively easy terms of peace that the world dictated. Its strength was that it did not try to put the clock back, and that it genuinely accepted the battle (Troeltsch), even though this ended with its defeat.

Defeat was followed by surrender, and by an attempt to make a completely fresh start based on the fundamentals of the Bible and the Reformation. Heim sought, along pietist and methodist lines, to convince the individual man that he was faced with the alternative, 'despair or Jesus'. He gained 'hearts'. Althaus (carrying forward the modern and positive line with a strong confessional emphasis) tried to wring from the world a place for Lutheran teaching (ministry) and Lutheran worship, and otherwise left the world to its own devices. Tillich set out to interpret the evolution of the world (against its will) in a religious sense – to give it its shape through religion. That was very brave of him, but the world unseated him and went on by itself; he, too, sought to understand the world better than it understood itself; but it felt that it was completely misunderstood and rejected the imputation. (Of course, the world *must* be understood better than it understands itself, but not 'religiously' as the religious socialists wanted.)

Barth was the first to realize the mistake that all these attempts (which were all, in fact, still sailing, though unintentionally, in the channel of liberal theology) were making in leaving clear a space for religion in the world or against the world. He brought in against religion the God of Jesus Christ, 'spirit against flesh'. That remains his greatest service. . . . Through his later dogmatics, he enabled the Church to effect this distinction, in principle, all along the line. It was not in ethics, as is often said, that he subsequently failed . . . it was that in the non-religious interpretation of theological concepts he gave no concrete guidance, either in dogmatics or ethics. There lies his limitation, and because of it his theology of revelation has become positivist, a 'positivism of revelation'.

The Confessing Church has forgotten all about the Barthian approach and has lapsed from positivism into conservative restoration. The important thing about that Church is that it carries on the great concepts of Christian theology; but it seems as if doing this is gradually just about exhausting it. It is true that there are in those concepts the elements of *genuine prophecy* (among them two things that you mention: the claim to truth and mercy) and of *genuine worship*; and to that extent the Confessing Church gets only attention, hearing and rejection. But both of them (prophecy and worship) remain undeveloped and remote, because there is no interpretation of them.

Bultmann seems to have somehow felt Barth's limitations, but he misconstrues them in the sense of liberal theology, and so goes off into the typical liberal process of reduction: the mythological elements of Christianity are dropped, and Christianity is reduced to its essence. My view is that the full content, including the mythological concepts, must be kept. The New Testament is not a mythological clothing of a universal truth; this mythology (resurrection, etc.) is the thing itself – but the concepts must be interpreted in such a way as not to make religion a precondition of faith. Only in that way, I think, will liberal theology be overcome and at the same time its question be genuinely taken up and answered. Thus the world's coming of age is no longer an occasion for polemics and apologetics, but is now really better understood than it understands itself, namely on the basis of the Gospel and in the light of Christ.

[*8 June 1944*][2]

THE HEALTHY MAN

Now I will try to go on with the theological reflections that I broke off not long since. I had been saying that God is being increasingly pushed out of a world that has come of age, out of the sphere of our knowledge and life. Theology has on the one hand resisted this development with apologetics and has taken up arms – in vain – against Darwinism, etc. On the other hand, it has accommodated itself to the development by restricting God to the so-called ultimate questions as a *deus ex machina*; that means he becomes the answer to life's problems, and the solution of its needs and conflicts. So, if anyone has no such difficulties, or if he refuses to go into these things, to allow others to pity him, then either he cannot be open to God; or else he must be shown that he is, in fact, deeply involved in such problems, needs and conflicts, without admitting or knowing it. If that can be done – and existentialist philosophy and psycho-therapy have worked out some quite ingenious methods in that direction – then this man can now be claimed for God, and methodism can celebrate its triumph. But if he cannot be brought to see and admit that his happiness is really an evil, his health sickness, and his vigour despair, the theologian is at his wits' end. It's a case of having to do either with a hardened sinner of a particularly ugly type or with a man of 'bourgeois complacency', and the one is as far from salvation as the other.

You see, that is the attitude that I am contending against. When Jesus blessed sinners, they were real sinners, but Jesus did not make everyone a sinner first. He called them away from their sin, not into their sin. It is true that encounter with Jesus meant the reversal of all human values. . . . It is true that Jesus cared about people on the fringes of society, such as harlots and tax-collectors, but never about them alone, for he sought to care about man as such. Never did he question a man's health, vigour or happiness . . . or regard them as evil fruits; or else why should he heal the sick and restore strength to the weak? Jesus claims for himself and the Kingdom of God the whole of human life in all its manifestations.

[*30 June 1944*][3]

PRIVATE AND PERSONAL

The displacement of God from the world, and from the public part
of human life, led to the attempt to keep his place secure in the
sphere of the 'personal', the 'inner', and the 'private'. And as every
man will have a private sphere somewhere, that is where he is
thought to be most vulnerable. . . . The range of his intimate life,
from prayer to his sexual life, have become the hunting ground of
modern pastoral workers. . . . From the sociological point of view,
this is a revolution from below. Just as the vulgar mind isn't satisfied
until it has seen some highly placed person 'in his bath', or in other
embarrassing situations, so it is here. There is a kind of evil satisfaction in knowing that everyone has his failings and weak spots. In my
contacts with the 'outcasts' of society, its 'pariahs', I've noticed
repeatedly that mistrust is the dominant motive in their judgement
of other people. Every action, even the most unselfish, of a person of
high repute is suspected from the outset. These 'outcasts' are to be
found in all grades of society. In a flower garden they grub around
only for the dung on which the flower grows. The more isolated a
man's life, the more easily he falls a victim to this attitude. There is
also a parallel isolation among the clergy, in what one might call the
'clerical' sniffing-around-after-people's-sins in order to catch them
out. It's as if you couldn't know a fine house till you had found a
cobweb in the furthest cellar, or as if you couldn't adequately appreciate a good play till you had seen how the actors behave off-stage.
It's the same kind of thing that you find in the novels of the last fifty
years, which do not think that they have depicted their characters
properly till they have described them in their marriage bed, or in
films where undressing scenes are thought necessary. Anything
clothed, veiled, pure and chaste is presumed to be deceitful,
disguised, and impure; people here simply show their own impurity.
A basic anti-social attitude of mistrust and suspicion is the revolt of
inferiority. Regarded theologically, the error is twofold: first, it is
thought that a man can be addressed as a sinner only after his weaknesses and meannesses have been spied out; secondly, it is thought
that a man's essential nature consists of his inmost and most intimate

background (that is defined as his 'inner life' and it is precisely in those secret human places that God is said to have his domain!).

On the first point, it has to be said that man is certainly a sinner, but is far from mean or common on that account. . . . It's not the sins of weakness, but the sins of strength that matter here. It's not in the least necessary to spy out things; the Bible never does.

Sins of Strength: in the genius, *hubris* (pride); in the peasant, the breaking of the order of life; in the bourgeois, fear of free responsibility. (Is this right?)

On the second point, the Bible does not recognize our distinction between the outward and the inward. Why should it? It is always concerned with *the whole man*, even where, as in the Sermon on the Mount, the decalogue is pressed home to refer to 'inward disposition'. That a good disposition can take the place of total goodness is quite unbiblical. The discovery of the so-called 'inner life' dates from the Renaissance, probably Petrach. The 'heart' in the biblical sense is not the inner life, but the whole man in relation to God. But as a man lives just as much from 'outwards' to 'inwards' as from 'inwards' to 'outwards', the view that his essential nature can be understood only from his intimate spiritual background is erroneous.

I therefore want to start from the premise that God shouldn't be smuggled in to some last secret place, but that we should frankly recognize that the world, and people, have come of age, that we shouldn't run man down in his worldliness, but confront him with God at his strongest point, that we should give up all our clerical tricks, and not regard psychotherapy and existentialist philosophy as God's pioneers. The importunity of all these people is far too unaristocratic for the Word of God to ally itself with them. The Word of God is far removed from this revolt of mistrust, this revolt from below. On the contrary, it reigns.

(By the way, it would be very nice if you didn't throw away my theological letters. Perhaps I might want to read them again later for work. One writes some things more freely and more vividly in a letter.)

[*8–9 July 1944.*][1]

A POEM

Who am I? They often tell me
I would step from my cell's confinement
calmly, cheerfully, firmly,
like a squire from his country house.

Who am I? They often tell me
I would talk to my warders
as though it were mine to command.

Who am I? They also tell me
I would bear the days of misfortune
equably, smilingly, proudly,
like one accustomed to win.

Am I then really all that which other men tell of?
Or am I only what I know of myself,
restless and longing and sick, like a bird in a cage,
struggling for breath, as though hands were compressing my
    throat
yearning for colours, for flowers, for the voices of birds,
thirsting for words of kindness, for neighbourliness,
trembling with anger at despotisms and petty humiliation,
tossing in expectation of great events,
powerlessly trembling for friends at an infinite distance,
weary and empty at praying, at thinking, at making,
faint and ready to say farewell to it all?

Who am I? This or the other?
Am I one person today, and tomorrow another?
Am I both at once? A hypocrite before others,
and before myself a contemptibly woebegone weakling?
Or is something within me still like a beaten army,
fleeing in disorder from victory already achieved?

Who am I? They mock me, these lonely questions of mine.
Whoever I am, thou knowest, O God, I am thine.

[*Sent to Eberhard Bethge with the letter of 9 July 1944.*][5]

EBERHARD BETHGE

AS IF GOD WERE NOT THERE

There is one great development which leads to the world's autonomy. In theology one sees it first in Lord Herbert of Cherbury, who maintains that reason is sufficient for religious knowledge. In ethics, it appears in Montaigne and Bodin with their substitution of rules of life for commandments. In politics Machiavelli detaches politics from morality in general and founds the doctrine of 'reasons of state'. Later and very different from Machiavelli, but tending like him towards the autonomy of human society, comes Grotius, setting up his natural law as international law, which is valid *etsi deus daretur* (even if God were not there). The philosophers provide the finishing touches: Descartes, Spinoza, Kant and Fichte and Hegel. Everywhere the thinking is directed towards the autonomy of man and the world. . . . God as a working hypothesis in morals, politics or science, has been surmounted and abolished; and the same thing has happened in philosophy and religion. For the sake of intellectual honesty, that working hypothesis should be dropped, or as far as possible eliminated. A scientist or physician who sets out to edify is a hybrid.

Anxious souls will ask what room there is left for God now; and as they know no answer to the question, they condemn the whole development that has brought them to such straits. I wrote to you before about the various emergency exits that have been contrived; and we ought to add to them the *salto mortale* (death leap) back into the Middle Ages. But the principle of the Middle Ages is heteronomy in the form of clericalism; a return to that can be a counsel of despair, and it would be at the cost of intellectual honesty. . . . There is no such way – at any rate not if it means deliberately abandoning our mental integrity; the only way is that of Matthew 18:3 (Unless you repent and become like children, you will never enter the kingdom of heaven), i.e., repentance through ultimate honesty. And we cannot be honest unless we recognize that we have to live in the world *etsi deus non daretur* (even if there were no God). And this is just what we do recognize – before God! God himself compels us to recognize it. So our coming of age leads us to a true recognition of our situation before God. God would have us know that we must live as men who manage our lives without him. The God who is with us is the God who forsakes us (Mark 15:34). The God who lets us live in the world without the working hypothesis of God is the God before whom we stand continually. Before God and with God we live without God. God lets himself be pushed out of the world on to the cross. He is weak and powerless in the world, and that is precisely the way in which he is with us and helps us. Matthew 8:17 ('He took our infirmities and bore our diseases') makes it quite clear that Christ helps us, not by virtue of his omnipotence, but by virtue of his weakness and suffering.

Here is the decisive difference between Christianity and all religions. Man's religiosity makes him look in his distress to the power of God in the world: God is the *deus ex machina*. The Bible directs man to God's powerlessness and suffering; only the suffering God can help. To that extent we can say that the development towards the world's coming of age . . . opens up a way of seeing the God of the Bible, who wins power and space in the world by his weakness. This will probably be the starting point for our 'secular' interpretation. [*16 July 1944*.][6]

A POEM

Men go to God when they are sore bestead,
Pray to him for succour, for his peace, for bread,
For mercy for them sick, sinning, or dead;
All men do so, Christian and unbelieving.

Men go to God when he is sore bestead,
Find him poor and scorned, without shelter or bread,
Whelmed under weight of the wicked, the weak, the dead;
Christians stand by God in his hour of grieving.

God goes to every man when sore bestead,
feeds body and spirit with his bread;
For Christians, pagans alike he hangs dead,
And both alike forgiving.

July 1944[7]

THE LAST MESSAGE TO THE BISHOP OF CHICHESTER

'For me it is the end but also the beginning – with him I believe in the principle of our universal Christian brotherhood which rises above all national interests and that our victory is certain – tell him too that I have never forgotten his words at our last meeting (i.e. in Sweden, Whitsuntide 1942).

[*Conveyed by Captain Payne Best of the British Secret Service, a fellow prisoner who survived.*][8]

* * *

Dietrich Bonhoeffer was executed at Flossenburg, 9 April 1945.

NOTES

Childhood and Youth

1. Eberhard Bethge, *Dietrich Bonhoeffer: A Biography, 1970*, pp. 24–25
2. Ibid, pp. 25–26
3. Ibid, pp. 39–41

America : 1930–1931

1. Ibid, pp. 72–81
2. *Love Letters from Cell 92*, p. 208

The Influence of Karl Barth

1. *No Rusty Swords*, pp. 114–18

A Pastor in Berlin

1. *No Rusty Swords*, pp. 120–27
2. Ibid, pp. 146–48

Theological Thoughts in the World Alliance

1. *No Rusty Swords*, pp. 153–69

A Voice for the Jews

1. *No Rusty Swords*, pp. 217–25
2. Ibid, pp. 226–27
3. Ibid, pp. 244–45

Pastorates in England: 1933–1935

1. *No Rusty Swords*, pp. 257–58
2. Ibid, pp. 261–73 (selected)
3. Ibid, pp. 284–87

Preachers' Seminary, Finkenwalde : 1935-1937

1. *No Rusty Swords*, pp. 296-302
2. *The Cost of Discipleship*, quoted by John de Gruchy in *Dietrich Bonhoeffer: Witness to Jesus Christ*, pp. 157-59
3. *No Rusty Swords*, complete text, pp. 321-39
4. *The Way to Freedom*, pp. 70-71
5. Ibid, complete text of correspondence, pp. 115-19

The Last Days of Finkenwalde

1. *The Way to Freedom*, pp. 137-43
2. Ibid, pp. 147-49
3. Ibid, pp. 72-74
4. Ibid, pp. 122-28
5. Ibid, pp. 199-202

The Safety and Security of America

1. *The Way to Freedom*, pp. 203-06
2. Ibid, pp. 214-17
3. Ibid, pp. 242-49

Pastoral Care in Wartime

1. *The Way to Freedom*, pp. 250-55
2. *True Patriotism*, pp. 28-33
3. Ibid, pp. 45-49

Conspirator and Pastor

1. *True Patriotism*, pp. 64-67
2. Ibid, pp. 69-96 (selected)
3. Ibid, pp. 122-26
4. Ibid, pp. 188-90
5. *Letters & Papers from Prison*, 1971, paragraphs from pp. 3-17

The Prisoner

1. *Letters and Papers from Prison*, pp. 31-32
2. *Love Letters from Cell 92*, pp. 12-13
3. *Letters and Papers from Prison*, pp. 33-35

4. Ibid, pp. 41-47 (the full text, from which selections have been made)
5. Ibid, pp. 70-72 (the full text — from which extracts have been taken)
6. *Love Letters from Cell 92*, pp. 52-54
7. *Love Letters from Cell 92*, pp. 87-88

Maria von Wedemeyer

1. *Love Letters from Cell 92*, p. 57
2. Ibid, pp. 64-65
3. Ibid, pp. 67-68
4. Ibid, pp. 79-80
5. Ibid, pp 94-97
6. Ibid, pp. 108-9
7. Ibid, pp. 167-69
8. Ibid, pp. 184-85
9. Ibid, pp. 192-93
10. Ibid, pp. 210-13
11. Ibid, p. 213

Eberhard Bethge

1. *Letters and Papers from Prison*, pp. 299-300
2. Ibid, pp. 325-29
3. Ibid, pp. 341-42
4. Ibid, pp. 344-47
5. Ibid, pp. 347-48
6. Ibid, pp. 359-61
7. Ibid, pp. 348-49
8. Lecture by Bishop of Chichester in Göttingen, May 1957.
   (*Gesammelten Schriften*, Vol. I, p. 412).